NEW DIRECTIONS FOR CHILD AND ADOLESCENT DEVELOPMENT

William Damon, *Stanford University*
EDITOR-IN-CHIEF

Enemies and the Darker Side of Peer Relations

Ernest V. E. Hodges
Noel A. Card
St. John's University

EDITORS

Number 102, Winter 2003

JOSSEY-BASS
San Francisco

ENEMIES AND THE DARKER SIDE OF PEER RELATIONS
Ernest V. E. Hodges, Noel A. Card (eds.)
New Directions for Child and Adolescent Development, no. 102
William Damon, Editor-in-Chief

Microfilm copies of issues and articles are available in 16mm and 35mm, as well as microfiche in 105mm, through University Microfilms Inc., 300 North Zeeb Road, Ann Arbor, Michigan 48106-1346.

ISSN 1520-3247   electronic ISSN 1534-8687

NEW DIRECTIONS FOR CHILD AND ADOLESCENT DEVELOPMENT is part of The Jossey-Bass Education Series and is published quarterly by Wiley Subscription Services, Inc., a Wiley company, at Jossey-Bass, 989 Market Street, San Francisco, California 94103-1741. Periodicals postage paid at San Francisco, California, and at additional mailing offices. Postmaster: Send address changes to New Directions for Child and Adolescent Development, Jossey-Bass, 989 Market Street, San Francisco, CA 94103-1741.

New Directions for Child and Adolescent Development is indexed in Biosciences Information Service, Current Index to Journals in Education (ERIC), Psychological Abstracts, and Sociological Abstracts.

SUBSCRIPTIONS cost $90.00 for individuals and $195.00 for institutions, agencies, and libraries.

EDITORIAL CORRESPONDENCE should be sent to the Editor-in-Chief, William Damon, Stanford Center on Adolescence, Cypress Building C, Stanford University, Stanford, CA 94305.

Cover photograph by Wernher Krutein/PHOTOVAULT © 1990.

Jossey-Bass Web address: www.josseybass.com

CONTENTS

EDITORS' NOTES

Peer relations have repeatedly been shown to play a significant role in personal, social, and academic development. At the group level, researchers have focused on both liking (peer acceptance or popularity) and disliking (peer rejection). More recently, attention has been focused on the role of dyadic relationships in development. Although much has been learned in recent years about the impact of positive dyadic relationships (that is, friendships) on child and adolescent development, the developmental significance of negative dyadic relationships has been largely ignored. This volume is intended to provide a conceptual and empirical basis for the study of these antipathetic relationships.

Theoretical and empirical attention is lacking regarding the formation and maintenance of antipathetic relationships. Are some youths more likely than others to become involved in inimical relationships? Children and adolescents who are aggressive or withdrawn, lack social skills, and have low cognitive ability are often rejected by the peer group, but these findings speak to disliking at the group level, and it is not clear that characteristics associated with peer rejection will necessarily be relevant to dyadic antipathy or enmities. How do enemy relationships form? Some may arise out of broken friendships, whereas others may emerge within the context of bully-victim relationships. It might also be expected that enmities could arise from jealousy (such as competition for a common friend or romantic partner) or through peer group structure (such as out-group biases and hostility). What distal factors, such as family environment and neighborhood characteristics, are relevant to the formation of enmity in the peer group? Are inimical relationships short-term or long-lasting? If they are long-lasting, what processes occur in the maintenance and solidification of these relationships? It might be expected that following the formation of an inimical relationship, certain behaviors, such as aggression and avoidance, biased perceptions, and high rates of retaliation, may maintain and intensify the enmity. Again, however, these possibilities have received little prior attention.

It might be expected that relationships based on mutual animosity have serious, often negative, developmental consequences for children and adolescents. As described by Abecassis in Chapter One, enmities are relationships based on hatred, hostility, and fear. Because enmities are relationships, in which by definition partners are unique from other peers, it is likely that this disdain is personalized, and perhaps more intense, than the unilateral dislike often examined when researchers talk of peer rejection. Moreover, children and adolescents who are not rejected at the group level may experience the same negative consequences associated with peer rejection by having a small number of enemies. It is also possible that those rejected at the group level differ in their developmental trajectories depending on whether peers' dislike toward them is unilateral or in the context of mutually antipathetic relationships. For these reasons, it might be expected that inimical relationships constitute a distinct developmental risk beyond that of peer rejection. However, the developmental consequences of enemies and other antipathetic relationships have received little prior attention.

This volume represents an effort to lay conceptual and empirical foundations for these previously unexplored topics. Using diverse samples, chapter authors provide an empirically based exposition of both distal (for example, attachment styles with parents, community violence exposure) and proximal (for example, perceptions of enemies' behavior, social structure of the peer group) factors related to inimical relationships. Developmental sequelae, such as affective, behavioral, and interpersonal, of having enemies are also explored within concurrent and longitudinal designs.

In Chapter One, Abecassis provides a typology of antipathetic relationships, of which enemy relationships are one type. She also provides an overview of prior theoretical and empirical work relevant to these negative relationships.

The second and third chapters explore how distal factors are related to inimical relationships with peers. In Chapter Two, Card and Hodges discuss associations between the family context and enmity within the peer group, and they present data on avoidant and preoccupied attachment styles to demonstrate these linkages in middle childhood. In Chapter Three, Schwartz, Hopmeyer-Gorman, Toblin, and Abou-ezzeddine demonstrate that children's inimical relationships with peers exacerbate associations between exposure to violence in the community and psychosocial adjustment in the peer group. These findings suggest that enmity with peers may provide contexts in which distal factors manifest as maladjustment.

Chapters Four through Six explore the processes and consequences of interpersonal enmity among children and early adolescents. In Chapter Four, Parker and Gamm examine individual behaviors and interpersonal adjustment associated with preadolescents' involvement in inimical relationships. The authors also demonstrate the potentially biased perceptions occurring within enmities, relative to friendships. Chapter Five, by Rodkin, Pearl, Farmer, and Van Acker, provides an examination of how the gender-segregated nature of children's peer groups manifests in antipathetic dyads. These authors also examine the temporal stability of children's inimical relationships, as well as co-occurring changes in behavioral and peer group adjustment. In Chapter Six, Pope examines the concurrent and longitudinal consequences associated with children's involvement in mutual antipathies, relative to the consequences associated with group-level rejection, contrasting two methodologies to assess inimical relationships.

In Chapter Seven, Hartup provides integration and commentary on the other chapters of this volume. More important, he suggests directions for future research in this emergent field. Using the definition of enemies suggested by Abecassis in Chapter One, Hartup also provides clarification of the constructs of enemies and mutual antipathies as they are used in the chapters of this volume.

The imperfect overlap between the conceptualization (Chapter One) and empirical operationalization (Chapters Two through Six) of enemy relationships, as Hartup points out in Chapter Seven, represents a clear call for researchers to better identify enemy relationships and distinguish them from other mutual antipathies when conducting work in this area. Many of the correlates of enemies reported in this volume are likely attenuated by confounding enemies and other mutual antipathies. That is, the processes and associated maladjustment studied here are likely to be operating more strongly within enemy relationships than other mutual antipathies. Future research with more precise assessment of enemy relationships might be expected to document better the developmental significance of child and adolescent enemies, as well as to explore differences in the processes involved in enemy and other antipathetic relationships.

In summary, this volume consists of theoretical and empirically based explorations of factors involved in the formation, maintenance, and impact of enemies and other mutual antipathies. These works are not meant to be authoritative, as it is likely that future research in this emergent area of study will clarify, and perhaps contradict, many of the findings reported here. Instead, our hope is that this volume will serve as a springboard for further theorizing and research on enemies and the darker side of peer relations.

Ernest V. E. Hodges
Noel A. Card
Editors

ERNEST V. E. HODGES is an associate professor of psychology at St. John's University, Jamaica, New York.

NOEL A. CARD is a doctoral candidate in clinical psychology at St. John's University, Jamaica, New York.

1

*The study of peers who dislike one another, termed
mutual antipathies, is being recognized as an important
aspect of a child's social world. An overview of this area
is provided, along with a focus on one particular type of
antipathy, enemies.*

I Hate You Just the Way You Are:
Exploring the Formation,
Maintenance, and Need for Enemies

Maurissa Abecassis

At one time or another, probably all of us have had a classmate, a boss, or
an acquaintance whom we did not like and were convinced that the feeling
was mutual. Although people may shy away from talking about these kinds
of relationships, they may not be rare. Negative emotion, aversion, avoidance, and even hatred are as central to the human experience as love, caring, and affiliation. *Antipathy* is a term used to refer to a broad category of
relationships, rooted in dislike and aversion, in which two peers recipro-
cally dislike one another (Abecassis, 1999). Inasmuch as friendships are
contexts for growth and development, the same can be said of mutual
antipathies. Antipathies—and enemies as one important type of antipathy—
are organizers of experience that inform us about a person's identity, moti-
vations, values, beliefs, emotions, and thoughts.

In the past several years, public awareness of antipathies has risen in
prominence. Antipathies are commonly discussed in the political arena
(particularly in the aftermath of the terrorist attacks of September 11, 2001),
in the world of sports, in both classic literary works and stories for children,
and in discussions about school shootings. Given the ubiquity of references
to antipathies, and to enmity more specifically, it is surprising that these
relationships have only recently begun to be studied. There are good reasons to be interested in studying all types of antipathies. One of them is an
emerging recognition that our understanding of the child's social world is
incomplete without knowledge of how "dark relationships" based on dislike and aversion are integrated into the child's social experience (Abecassis,

NEW DIRECTIONS FOR CHILD AND ADOLESCENT DEVELOPMENT, no. 102, Winter 2003   © Wiley Periodicals, Inc.

1999). Furthermore, there may be several different kinds of "dark" relationships that have yet to be studied, the most interesting of which is enmity.

Are Enemy Relationships Distinct from Mutual Antipathies?

The term *mutual antipathy* has been used to describe a broad category of relationships whose unifying characteristic is a basis of reciprocated dislike (Abecassis, 1999; Abecassis and others, 2002). For the most part, empirical efforts to identify mutual antipathies have used sociometric nominations more than rating tasks. In some studies, children have been asked to identify three peers whom they "do not like to play with" or "work with" (Hembree and Vandell, 1999; Chapter Two, this volume), and in other studies, children have been asked to nominate three peers whom they "dislike more than anyone else" (Hayes, Gershman, and Bolin, 1980), "like least" (Chapters Three and Five, this volume), or "do not like at all" (Abecassis and others, 2002). A child is categorized as involved in a mutual antipathy if that child, among his or her three choices, nominated a peer as "not liked at all," for example, and the child's classmate reciprocated the nomination. A further distinction has been drawn between same-sex antipathies, which involve reciprocated nominations between peers of the same sex, and mixed-sex antipathies, which involve reciprocated nominations between children of the opposite sex (Abecassis and others, 2002). This distinction has proven to be very fruitful in elucidating the role that gender plays in understanding the correlates of antipathy involvement for boys and girls (Abecassis and others, 2002; Chapter Five, this volume).

In the hypothetical example in Figure 1.1, three children are asked to nominate "three peers you do not like at all." Those who nominate one another have a mutual antipathy. By this measure, Chelsea and Tim are both involved in one mutual antipathy, and Sandra is involved in two mutual antipathies: one with Chelsea (a same-sex antipathy) and one with Tim (mixed-sex). It is assumed that the other children nominated by Chelsea, Tim, and Sandra did not reciprocate the nominations. Although we have asserted that these children have mutual antipathies, we cannot yet categorize the type of antipathy they share—whether based on the loss of friendship, bullying and victimization, competitors, or simple aversion. Even after knowing the basis for the antipathy, we would still need to determine if each child in an antipathy dyad perceives the peer's negative sentiments. If both children in the dyad recognize the sentiment, we could regard it as a true enmity from which hatred is likely to follow. If, however, one of the peers in the dyad does not recognize the antipathy, we should regard it as unilateral, and the feelings could range from mild aversion (for the child who does not recognize the antipathy) to hatred for the peer who does. For peers who do not perceive the antipathy, it is a nonrelationship.

Conceptually, mutual antipathies are best thought of as a broad category that incorporates relationships that share a common basis of dislike but are likely to be heterogeneous in a variety of other ways. For example, mutual antipathies may differ in terms of perceived mutuality, strength and intensity of feelings, correlates of involvement, origins, and developmental course of these relationships. Some antipathies, for example, may involve simple aversion, while others may involve greater dislike or even hatred. Some antipathies may develop between peers who do not know one another well, while others may develop between well-acquainted peers or even former friends. Some types of mutual antipathies may involve avoidance, and others may involve increased interaction or even aggression. Some dyads

Figure 1.1. Nomination Method for Identifying Mutual Antipathies Among Peers

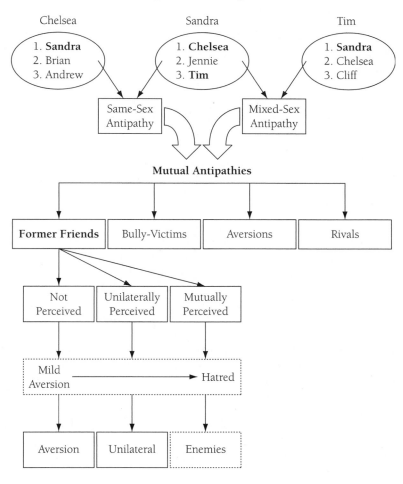

classified as involved in an antipathy may recognize the existence of an antipathy, and other dyads may be unaware. Whether unilateral or mutual, both types of antipathies are worthy of further study, although one-sided relationships may differ from mutual ones in terms of the nature of interaction and quality of these relationships (see Hartup, Laursen, Stewart, and Eastenson, 1988).

Antipathies, as illustrated in Figure 1.1, are best regarded as a superordinate class that encompasses a variety of relationships that may include (but are not limited to) the following types: some bully-victim dyads, rivals or competitors, former friends, and children who simply feel some aversion toward one another.

Some of these dyads may involve antipathies, others enmities, and yet others may be neither (children who nominate one another yet feel no strong sense of dislike). For enmity, dislike is a necessary but not sufficient condition, since it is possible to dislike someone more than anyone else and not regard that person as an enemy (Abecassis, 1999). Thus, being enemies constitutes the most extreme or intense form of antipathy characterized by hatred rather than mere dislike. From this perspective, any of the antipathies identified in Figure 1.1 could be enmities if they involved dyads that hate rather than dislike one another.

Empirically, current methods do not allow enemies to be distinguished from other kinds of mutual antipathies. Conceptually, theorizing about the nature of enemies is well elaborated, suggesting that enemies are dangerous, malicious, and unfriendly peers who engage in hostile acts or pose a significant danger or threat to well-being, aims, and goals, while endorsing different beliefs and values (Holt, 1989; Middents, 1994; Shallit, 1988). An enemy's gain is perceived to be our loss (Shallit, 1989; Beck, 1999). Because enemies dominate one another's actions, thoughts, and feelings, members of these dyads feel preoccupied with feelings of fear and hatred for one's enemy (Rieber and Kelly, 1991).

Enemies can be considered more or less evil and threatening depending on how disliked the enemy is (ranging from disliked to hated), how active the enemy is in trying to cause trouble, who the enemy is (a work associate, friend, or peer), how much contact one must have with an enemy, how aware a person is of his or her enemies (that is, whether the feeling is mutual or unilateral), and whether enemies are symmetric or asymmetric in power and status (Wiseman and Duck, 1995; Beck, 1999; Abecassis, 1999). Equally powerful enemies, for example, may be perceived as especially challenging and threatening, which may serve to keep aggression at a minimum. Asymmetries in power may be especially motivating for a peer interested in defeating a more powerful enemy—sort of a David and Goliath complex.

In sum, antipathies incorporate a broad set of heterogeneous relationships rooted in dislike. Enmity, the most intense type of antipathy, is characterized by strong feelings of hatred. Although very little empirical work on enemy relationships exists, studies of mutual antipathy alluded to in this chapter, and elaborated on by other chapter authors, serve as the starting point for the study of enemies. If we hypothesize that enemy relationships involve some of the same processes that occur in the formation of an antipathy, we can think of studies of mutual antipathy as providing us with a liberal estimate of the prevalence and nature of enmities.

An Overview of the Empirical Findings on Mutual Antipathies

One of the most basic questions about antipathies relates to their prevalence. Among preschool children, evidence of antipathy involvement has not yet been found, though there is clear evidence of antipathy involvement in middle childhood and adolescence, with most children involved in only one antipathy at any given time (Hayes and others, 1980; Abecassis and others, 2002). Involvement in antipathies is found across all sociometric groups with elevated rates of involvement among rejected children (Abecassis and others, 2002; Chapters Five and Six, this volume). Rates of antipathy involvement, however, vary widely across studies with estimates as follows: 65 percent of third-grade children (Hembree and Vandell, 1999), between 15 and 40 percent of third- and fourth-grade children (Chapter Five, this volume), 29 percent of children in third through fifth grade (Chapter Three, this volume), 33 percent of children in third through sixth grade (Chapter Six, this volume), 48 percent of children in fourth through eighth grade (Chapter Two, this volume), and 58 percent of seventh- through ninth-grade children (Chapter Four, this volume).

Most studies (with the exception of those reported in Chapters Five and Six, this volume, and Abecassis and others, 2002) have not distinguished between same-sex (SS) and mixed-sex (MS) antipathy involvement. In a recent study based on a sample of Dutch children and adolescents, we reported that SS antipathy involvement is more common among boys (roughly 25 percent) in middle childhood compared to girls (roughly 8 percent), though the disparity decreased in adolescence (Abecassis and others, 2002). MS antipathy involvement was comparable among boys and girls in both middle childhood and adolescence (roughly at 15 to 17 percent; Abecassis and others, 2002). Overall, the prevalence of mutual antipathies allows us to deduce that rates of enmity are likely much lower than rates of antipathy involvement.

In general, antipathy involvement is associated with a variety of negative behavioral outcomes. After accounting for peer rejection status, SS antipathy involvement was associated with antisocial behavior and social withdrawal in childhood and adolescence and to emotionality and a lack of friendship support in adolescence (Abecassis and others, 2002). MS antipathy involvement was associated with a very different pattern of behavior among boys and girls. Among boys, it was associated with antisocial behavior and bullying, and among girls, with nonaggressiveness, victimization, depression, and less prosocial behavior (Abecassis and others, 2002).

While further evidence is accumulating that involvement in antipathies is correlated with a variety of behavioral indicators, we used a longitudinal sample of Dutch children to examine the stability of involvement in antipathies over time and the extent to which involvement in antipathies in middle childhood could aid in the prediction of social behavior in adolescence. Evaluating the long-term impact of these relationships helps to establish the developmental significance of these relationships.

Using a longitudinal Dutch sample of 398 children, tested at age eleven and again three years later, we found that 53 percent of boys and 42 percent of girls were involved in an antipathy in childhood or adolescence, or both time points (Abecassis and others, 2002). For most children, though, involvement in antipathies usually occurred at only one point in time, though boys (10 percent), more often than girls (5 percent), were involved in antipathies in both childhood and adolescence. Rodkin and others (Chapter Five, this volume) suggest that when involvement in antipathies is examined longitudinally, children tend not to be involved in antipathies with the same child over time.

In a series of regression analyses, I examined the extent to which involvement in SS and MS antipathies in childhood could aid in the prediction of social behavior in adolescence even after related baseline measures (including peer rejection) were included in the analyses (Abecassis, 1999). For boys only, involvement in SS antipathies (but not MS antipathies), in addition to a set of baseline measures, aided in the prediction of a socially reserved or withdrawn behavior pattern—for example, noninvolvement in addictive behaviors and delinquency, lack of parental support, and lack of support for autonomy. Involvement in SS antipathies in childhood predicts a very different pattern of behavior in adolescence compared to the concurrent correlates of involvement in antipathies. Although these findings are preliminary and require more in-depth study, they suggest that SS antipathy involvement may have a long-term impact on a child's social functioning. Further work will be needed to examine whether SS or MS antipathy involvement may affect a different set of behaviors in girls.

Evidence is accumulating that antipathies do relate to important behavioral indicators that may have a long-term impact on children, though this requires further support. Important avenues for further work are suggested by the findings in this volume, which emphasize the need to consider immediate contexts, such as the family (see Chapter Two, this volume) and peer group (see Chapters Four and Six, this volume), as well as wider contextual influences like community violence (see Chapter Three, this volume). Distinguishing between SS and MS antipathies will continue to be important. The need to refine the identification and measurement of antipathies and enemies is also clear.

Methodological Issues in the Study of Antipathies and Enemies

Limitations of the current methods of measuring antipathies argue strongly for the use of multiple measures carefully constructed to use a stricter set of criteria to categorize antipathies and obtain more detailed information about the strength and intensity of dislike and hatred in an effort to distinguish enemies from antipathies. Because obtaining permission to ask children to name their enemies may be difficult, identifying enemies unequivocally will continue to remain a challenge. Several recommendations are made for improving and expanding on existing measures.

The use of a consistent protocol for identifying antipathies will be essential for ensuring comparability across studies. Asking children to nominate three peers whom they "do not like at all" or "dislike more than anyone else" may be more valid measures for accurately assessing the experience of dislike or hatred compared to more general questions that ask children to name peers they "do not like to play with." Greater consistency and accuracy in estimating the prevalence of enemies and antipathies would be a likely result of using one of these two sociometric questions.

Using nomination tasks in conjunction with rating tasks will also improve classification. One way to use rating and nomination methods to yield additional information would be to classify children involved in a mutual antipathy based on the order (first, second, or third) in which a child names a peer in the nomination task and whether a peer reciprocates the nomination in the same order and the sociometric ratings of each child's peers using a five-point scale (with 1 meaning "not like at all"). Information about the strength or intensity of an antipathy may be obtained based on the order in which a child names a peer. Using the example in Figure 1.1, is the antipathy between Chelsea and Sandra, who both name each other in the first position, stronger than the antipathy between Tim and Sandra? It is reasonable to assume that a link may exist between the order of a child's nomination and the strength of aversion. Children who have a mutual antipathy based on the nomination task and rate their peer as a 1 or 2 on the rating tasks would be classified as having a mutual antipathy. The need to understand the relation between rating and nomination tasks better is made by Pope (Chapter Six, this volume), whose findings suggest that sociometric ratings yield higher estimates of antipathy involvement than nomination tasks do.

Another way to improve the chances of identifying enemies is by including additional items along with the nomination and rating questions. Once a child gives a peer a low sociometric rating and nominates that same peer as disliked, the child would be asked to complete additional ratings of the relationship with the peer, which might include such questions as: How close do you feel to this peer? How much time do you spend with this peer? How much do you avoid this peer? How much time do you spend thinking about this peer? Ratings across a variety of cognitive and behavioral questions might give some indication of the strength and nature of the animosity.

Another way of gaining similar information about the strength and intensity of antipathies and enemies would be to develop a "president or prime minister for the day" sociometric interview. Students might be asked to imagine being president or prime minister for the day and being able to make judgments for their peers. Children could be presented with the following kinds of scenarios:

- You are allowed to take your classmates to an amusement park, but you have the power to decide if some children have to stay at school. Name three peers whom you would want to stay at school and miss the day of fun at the park.
- You are stranded on a desert island. Which three of your classmates would you hate to get stuck with on the island?

This approach, if used with younger children, in conjunction with sociometric ratings and nominations of mutual antipathies, might yield corroborating information on the strength of a child's feelings about nominated peers.

With current methods of identifying antipathies, we infer that children categorized as "involved in an antipathy" feel dislike for one another and realize that they have a mutual antipathy with a peer: that is, they dislike a peer and know the peer dislikes them. Without evidence of this mutuality, one could argue that in theory, these antipathies are mutual (from a measurement standpoint), but in practice, dyads that lack a perception of mutuality are at best unilateral antipathies in some cases and nonrelationships in others. Mutuality may be assessed by asking children to "name three peers who do not like you at all" and comparing those responses with those of their peers, as has been done in previous studies (MacDonald and Cohen, 1995). If a child is identified as "involved in a mutual antipathy" and is accurate in perceiving which peer dislikes him, it is a good indicator of the mutuality of the relationship.

Finally, using multiple informants may be helpful in gathering additional evidence for classifying children involved in antipathies or enmities and learning about how these relationships are perceived by others. Teacher, parent, and peer reports may be used in conjunction with sociometric tests to confirm a child's involvement in an antipathy. In fact, Parker and Gamm (Chapter Four, this volume) provide evidence that children have more negative perceptions of their enemies than do other peers. Although using multiple measures often does not yield consistent data, this information gives a sense of the extent to which others recognize the existence of antipathies. Finally, observation is unlikely to be effective for studying these relationships since interaction between children in a mutual

antipathy or enemy relationship may be very infrequent and, unlike affiliation, avoidance is hard to measure and may have multiple meanings.

The studies of mutual antipathy described in this volume lay the
groundwork for further work in this area. Thus far, it has not been possible
to differentiate among types of antipathies or to establish the actual experience of shared animosity unequivocally. Because many studies of mutual
antipathy have grown out of existing data sets, new investigations will allow
for the refinement of methods used to study antipathies and, ultimately,
enemies. In the last half of this chapter, consideration is given to how and
why enemy relationships develop.

How Do We Form Enemy Relationships?

Prevalence rates of mutual antipathies suggest that enemy development may
be uncommon among preschool and young school-age children and become
more common among middle school children and adolescents (Hayes and
others, 1980; Hembree and Vandell, 1999; Abecassis and others, 2002). The
development of enemy relationships is likely to depend on several attain-
ments, including a cognitive understanding of what an enemy is, exposure
to enemies or enemy images in the media, and general changes in cognitive
development that affect the development of peer relationships and expectations of these relationships, such as decreased egocentrism, perspective-
taking abilities, and development of one's self-concept (Hartup and
Abecassis, 2002; Harter, 1990; Bigelow, 1977; Hesse and Mack, 1991).

Enemy relationships may develop when some aspect of a person's
social image or status is challenged (Beck, 1999). An innocuous event
occurs—perhaps an offhand remark about friendliness is made—and if this
event touches on an area of uncertainty or vulnerability (the person may
wonder, *Am I unfriendly?*), the remark may be personalized. Personalization
refers to a process by which an individual interprets an action or comment
as directed at or specifically referring to him or her (Beck, 1999). When an
event is personalized, the "offended" individual may assume that the comment was intentional and assume that the other person holds a negative
view of her (she thinks, *I'm unfriendly*). According to Beck (1999), these
slights, offending events, or comments can be real or imagined. The
offended person adopts a cognitive set in which the offender's motives are
recast as malicious, dangerous, evil, or threatening and she may search
memory for past evidence of real or imagined violations. What starts out
initially as distress or hurt feelings is transformed into a sense of having
been wronged, which leads to feelings of anger and strong dislike or hatred,
as well as a desire to attack in response and to preserve a sense of self.

In the absence of an interest or willingness to be introspective (*Maybe
I am an unfriendly person, and the comment was accurate*) and consider
whether an action was personally directed (*Was that comment really about
me?*) or to communicate with the "offender" to express the hurt, the risk of

developing an enemy relationship is increased. The "offended person" may avoid her enemy, behave rudely (with nonverbal behaviors such as sneers and slights), or return negative comments. Now "the offender" may notice these slights and start to interact differently with the initially offended peer. If a mutual enmity is to develop, the offender may be drawn into the relationship by scrutinizing her peer's behavior and also take offense. Alternatively, the "offender" may choose to ignore, overlook, or decrease interaction with her peer and interpret her behavior with a situational attribution (*She's having a really hard day today*) instead of a dispositional one (*She is a mean and nasty person*), and a unilateral enmity may result.

Cognitive processing biases support the development and continued existence of enmity between peers. First, people often attribute the development of an enemy relationship to their enemy and claim that they had nothing to do with its onset (Wiseman and Duck, 1995). This self-serving bias allows a person to attribute the development of an enemy relationship solely to the enemy, absolving himself of any role in the process. Second, once a person is categorized as an enemy, people expect future hostile actions, and each facet of information processing (encoding, interpretation of social cues, clarification of goals, selection of a response, and enacting the response) is then affected by this expectation (Crick and Dodge, 1994). Parker and Gamm (Chapter Four, this volume) provide some support for this process.

These processes can happen between friends or between peers who do not know one another well. What is unclear is how often this process of personalization and projection needs to occur for enmity to develop, whether there are some particular areas of sensitivity that have a greater likelihood of eliciting this response, and whether we can identify periods of heightened sensitivity to misperceptions (for example, times of transition). Most people engage in this process of personalization and projection at one time or another (Beck, 1999). Some people, however, may be more susceptible to this pattern of processing and to the development of enmities.

Personal Characteristics That Increase the Susceptibility to Enmity. A variety of situational factors (such as a child's attachment history) undoubtedly contribute to the heightened sensitivity that leads to the development of an enemy relationship (see Chapter Two, this volume), but some other personal characteristics may also affect susceptibility to developing these relationships.

Relational aggression (RA) is defined as a pattern of aggressive behavior, used more frequently by girls, to cause harm to others' relationships through such behavior as the use of exclusionary tactics, rumors, gossip, and threats (Crick, 1995). Because enemies depend on subtle nonverbal behavior, such as slights, ignoring a peer, or trying to get others to dislike a peer, RA may typify children who are prone to develop antipathies (Holt, 1989; Wiseman and Duck, 1995). All of these behaviors are consistent with activities that relationally aggressive children use on peers (Crick, 1995).

Because gender is an important facet in understanding antipathies, a link between enmity and RA is plausible and has already received some support in a recent study (Chapter Four, this volume).

Reactive aggression is an angry response to frustration or provocation, in which children attribute hostile intent to the actions of others even in ambiguous situations (Crick and Dodge, 1996). The reactively aggressive child may interpret peers' actions as motivated by hostile intent, and he perceives his peers as mean and threatening to the self, which may make these children more likely to develop antipathies (Crick and Dodge, 1996). These children rarely afford peers the benefit of the doubt when interpreting behavior, and hostility is assumed on the part of peers, which may draw peers into enemy relationships. Interpreting a peer's behavior as hostile, becoming angry, and retaliating against the peer may lead the peer to respond aggressively (or avoid the child) in kind (Crick and Dodge, 1996). These patterns support the process of enemy development that Beck (1999) proposed.

Children who have a special sensitivity to cues of rejection may be especially attuned to the comments of peers. Rejection sensitivity (RS) refers to a pattern of behavior in which a person is predisposed to expect, perceive, and react intensely to actual or perceived rejection due to a history of being rejected (Purdie and Downey, 2000). Children and adults who show this tendency search for cues of rejection and show intense hostile reactions to perceived or actual rejection. RS children respond to ambiguous rejection (for example, "No, I can't go with you," in response to a proffered invitation) with angry thoughts, feelings, and action plans (Purdie and Downey, 2000). Children who are RS show special sensitivity to cues of rejection even when they do not exist, making them especially susceptible to overinterpreting social cues.

Although a greater proportion of rejected children tend to have antipathies, children of all sociometric categories have them, and it would seem that the same is true for enemies (Abecassis and others, 1999; Hembree and Vandell, 1999). The reasons for or factors that precipitate enmity, however, may differ for children of different sociometric classifications. Popular children, for example, are less accurate at perceiving who dislikes them, but their high social status may make them good choices as enemies (MacDonald and Cohen, 1995). Controversial children, who receive many like and dislike nominations and are also high in status, appear to have a combination of prosocial and aggressive behavior patterns that may make them especially likely to have enemies (Dodge, 1983).

Empirical Support for the Process of Enemy Formation. Several empirical studies lend support to this account of enemy development. In two studies, participants were asked to indicate if they believed they had an enemy and how that relationship had developed (Holt, 1989; Wiseman and Duck, 1995). While rates of enemy involvement were quite high, with 70 percent of adults reporting current or past involvement in an enmity, reasoning about the causes was vague. The development of an enmity was perceived to be surprising and unanticipated and was precipitated by the detection of a bad feeling from their peer, rude nonverbal behavior (such as slights, sneers, and dirty looks), or a realization about how their "enemy" treated them compared to others (Holt, 1989; Wiseman and Duck, 1995). Designation of enemy status came only after an overt and unanticipated hostile act occurred—for example, an insult, showing disregard for one's feelings, or being rejected, socially excluded, or ignored (Holt, 1989; Wiseman and Duck, 1995).

Additional support for this account comes from studies that suggest that people may be drawn into enmities because they prefer a state of symmetry between how much they like or dislike a peer and how much that peer likes or dislikes them (Blumberg, 1969; Curtis and Miller, 1986). In a series of studies, Blumberg (1969) examined how comfortable people feel in relationships that are symmetrical and asymmetrical in feeling (for example, liking someone the same as, more than, or less than he or she likes you). Overwhelmingly, participants preferred symmetry in these relationships, even if that meant a decrease in the other person's liking. For example, they preferred to be disliked by a person whom they disliked (Blumberg, 1969). This preference for equity may help to explain why some children and adults are drawn into enemy relationships. It is important to note, however, that it is not clear if a preference for equity exists with extreme negative emotions such as hatred.

Once a person believes that another dislikes him, his behavior is likely to change. When adults are led to believe that a peer they had interacted with and with whom they were to interact with again liked or disliked them, the adults behaved in ways that confirmed expectations (Curtis and Miller, 1986). Adults who believed they were disliked showed less warmth, disagreed more, and expressed more dissimilarity toward the peer who "disliked" them. These reactions were exacerbated for individuals who had lower self-esteem and perceived themselves as less likeable.

Taken together, theoretical and empirical findings support the premise that enemy relationships may be initiated in a climate of misperception. Once an act or event is perceived as offensive, the offended party assumes intentionality, and in the absence of discussion or introspection, the victim may behave in ways that signal dislike or hatred of the peer. Information processing biases and mechanisms serve to support this process (Crick and Dodge, 1994).

How Do We Keep Our Enemies?

Being enemies, at least on the surface, appears to provide few rewards. If these relationships are so unpleasant, what supports and fosters their continued existence?

Although little is known about how children and adults interact with enemies, there is some indication that these relationships depend on limited interaction for their continued existence. Adults who had an enemy felt uncomfortable, tense, guarded, vigilant, and unable to speak in their enemy's presence (Wiseman and Duck, 1995). Given this complex of feelings, it is not surprising that enemies choose to minimize contact, avoid one another when possible, present false fronts, or use other peers to buffer their effect (Holt, 1989; Wiseman and Duck, 1995).

A handful of cognitive processing studies support the view that children and adults believe that enemies communicate very little, and when they do, the interactions are expected to be uncooperative and ineffective. In one study, children were asked to indicate how they would make a request of a friend or enemy (Bernicot and Mahrokhian, 1989). Hints (for example, "Gee, that toy looks like it would be fun to play with") and justifications were used instead of direct requests, suggesting that these strategies are used when the person being addressed is perceived to be uncooperative (Bernicot and Mahrokhian, 1989). In a similar study, adults reported on the persuasion strategies used with friends, fathers, or enemies to gain information, change an opinion, or get someone to do something (Rule, Bisanz, and Kohn, 1985). With enemies, participants reported that there were few issues on which they would try to persuade an enemy. Persuasion attempts, when they did occur, were focused on trying to convince enemies to harm themselves or others, make fools of themselves, go away, or commit a crime (Rule and others, 1985). These findings are consistent with the general sense of helplessness people report over the development and amelioration of these relationships (Wiseman and Duck, 1995; Holt, 1989).

Once a peer is categorized as an enemy, children show a pattern of attributing the most hostile and negative motives to this person. In one study, children read scenarios in which they evaluated a victim's attributions when a best friend, acquaintance, or enemy committed an act that was accidental, ambiguous, or hostile in intent (Ray and Cohen, 1997). In ambiguous and even accidental situations, children evaluated the enemy's intent less positively than that of best friends or acquaintances; children expected the victim would be more likely to retaliate against an enemy. Children also reported very low levels of liking for enemies across contexts. In a follow-up study, children evaluated the intent of friends, enemies, and acquaintances in one of two conflict contexts. In the "peer group entry" context a target child approached a group of peers and tried to join in play. In the "limited resource" context, two children were trying to gain access to the same computer game (Ray and Cohen, 2000). Once again, children judged the intentions of enemies more negatively than those of friends or acquaintances, especially for the peer group entry situation. In other studies, peers perceived their enemies more negatively than the rest of the peer group did on valued tasks and in terms of a variety of behavioral measures such as aggressiveness, jealousy, and prosocial behavior (Tesser, Campbell, and Smith, 1984; Chapter Four, this volume).

In some ways, enemy relationships may be easier to maintain than to extinguish. Several suggestions for resolving enmities have been suggested. In an effort to preserve self-esteem and stop worrying about one's enemy, one might continue a pattern of avoidance (Wiseman and Duck, 1995). By talking with friends, these participants hoped to achieve respect and establish credibility about their account of the situation. Denying the situation and trying to ignore the situation and pretend it did not exist was another approach cited by some adults with enemies (Wiseman and Duck, 1995; Beck, 1999). Two of the less adaptive approaches were to find (or create) another enemy who is perceived to be even more threatening to take the place of the current enemy or try to defeat one's enemy (Shallit, 1988). Finally, although one group of adults espoused a desire to resolve their enmity by discussing it with their enemy, they reported that this approach was unsuccessful (Wiseman and Duck, 1995). Acknowledgment of one's role in the formation of an enmity may indicate reflective capacity and be an important first step in breaking the cycle of enmity (Wiseman and Duck, 1995; Beck, 1999).

One of the most interesting suggestions for resolving enemy relationships comes from the classic work of Sherif and others in the Robber's Cave study (1961). By separating two groups of boys at a summer camp and fostering separate group identities, friendships across groups were severed and intergroup hostility fostered. When group members were forced to interact to achieve a shared goal, hostility and animosity decreased. This work provides a hopeful suggestion for intervention and resolution of enmities by allowing enemies to interact in a structured setting to achieve a shared goal. Although allowing children who are enemies to remain separate and avoid interaction may seem to be a way to keep the peace, this separation may perpetuate and maintain these relationships.

Taken together, these studies suggest that people with enemies do not enjoy interacting with their enemies, and when considering the actions of enemies, the worst is always assumed, with positive information minimized and greater weight placed on negative information (Holt, 1989; Wiseman and Duck, 1995; Ray and Cohen, 1997). Resolving enmities is especially challenging since it often involves resolving the relationship in the absence of dialogue.

Do We Need Enemies?

The reasons for developing close personal friendships are clear, and the developmental significance of having friends has been discussed extensively elsewhere (Hartup, 1996). Studies of mutual antipathies suggest that involvement in these relationships is associated with a variety of negative emotional and behavioral indicators described earlier in this chapter and throughout this volume (see also Hembree and Vandell, 1999; Abecassis and others, 2002). If involvement in enmities is associated with poorer adjustment, then why have these relationships? What function do they serve?

Clearly in some circumstances, having an enemy may be stressful and challenging. But there are likely other instances in which having an enemy is exciting, organizing, and motivating. For example, enmities may serve to make a child's other peer relationships more cohesive. Friendships, as a context that provides support, self-disclosure, intimacy, and sharing may also help to buffer and protect children with enemies (Berndt and Perry, 1986). Because mutual friends share behavioral similarities and hold similar views of peers, those with enemies may call on their friends to confirm their view of the enemy, share in the hatred, and behave similarly toward the enemy. Because enemies are perceived as threatening and malicious, having a peer "on your side" may help children manage these relationships by providing a sympathetic ear to process an enemy's perceived offenses. Enmity can also improve the bonds of friendship: friends can band together, share views on an enemy, and support one another as they disparage the enemy. Some evidence suggests that adults do in fact count on their friends for this kind of support (Wiseman and Duck, 1995). A child might seek out other peers for friendship who are known to dislike one's enemy. The adage "my enemy's enemy is my friend" captures this notion best. If friendships serve as a buffer for children and adults with enemies and become stronger as a result, then those who are involved in enemy relationships and lack mutual friendships may be especially at risk.

The need for enemies may be most deeply tied to an individual's need to develop an integrated sense of self. Perhaps the most important function of enemies is to help children (and adults) deal with unacceptable parts of the self. Psychoanalytically oriented theorists have argued that the developmental need for enemies, or objects of hatred, begins quite early in an effort to externalize unacceptable aspects of the self and preserve a sense of self with which one can identify (Boyer, 1986; Volkan, 1985). The origins of this process are thought to begin in infancy, with the differentiation of self that occurs in the attachment relationship, linked in important ways with the need for enemies (Volkan, 1985). As a child begins to conceptualize a consistent sense of self, qualities are dichotomized in bipolar ways (for example, good versus bad and pleasurable versus unpleasurable), and to help in the integration of these contrary views of self, externalizing these negative feelings and projecting them on to an enemy is one way to manage conflictual feelings. This process of externalization is similar in concept to projection or projective identification (Boyer, 1986; Beck, 1999). Positive feelings support the emergence of a cohesive sense of self, but aggressive feelings or negative aspects of the self threaten the cohesion unless they are kept at a distance and used as a comparison (Volkan, 1985; Boyer,

1986; Higgins, 1987). This is essentially what happens when a peer assumes the worst of an enemy even though other peers view the "enemy" with greater equanimity (Chapter Four, this volume; Tesser and others, 1981). Enmity emanates from within and allows the individual to manage negative feelings about one's self by endowing or projecting on to the enemy these unacceptable parts. Furthermore, enemies can be motivating; children and adults may enjoy having an enemy to compete against. Striving to "defeat" an enemy may help them strive to defeat the disliked parts of self.

By implication, the selection of an enemy is not random. The characteristics of an enemy are of central importance. In selecting an enemy, one might choose a person who possesses (1) traits or characteristics that one has but dislikes (similarity), (2) traits that one has but that another possesses to a greater degree (similarity), (3) traits that one envies or wishes he or she had but does not have (dissimilarity), or (4) traits that are disliked that one does not have (dissimilarity). Further research will need to assess these possibilities and determine whether people are aware of the differences or similarities that may exist with an enemy.

In "hating" one's enemy, one is also permitted to "hate" aspects of the self. Having an enemy and working through this relationship may enable a child or adult to foster greater self-knowledge, the development of empathy, or social feeling and an ability to take the perspective of the other (Beck, 1999). As Rieber and Kelly (1991, p. 33) put it, "The psychologically well integrated individual is aware of his own vices; he does not need to invent enemies or to project his own evil outside of himself."

Conclusion

If it is not politically incorrect to say, this is an exciting time for those interested in studying the development of enmities and antipathies. Studies of mutual antipathy described in this volume provide clear evidence that involvement in antipathies is fairly common, that these relationships have important developmental implications, and that new studies using improved methods can offer greater clarity in understanding whether different kinds of antipathies can be distinguished and how prevalent they are. Studies of mutual antipathy may provide important clues about how enmities work. Enemy relationships may be the most intense and extreme type of antipathy, with some shared commonality in the developmental processes of these relationships. If this is the case, then findings on mutual antipathies and the processes identified in those studies may be similar but stronger in the case of enmities. The study of enmities will benefit from the continued refinement of the methods used to assess these relationships.

References

Abecassis, M. "I Dislike You and You Dislike Me: Prevalence and Developmental Significance of Mutual Antipathies Among Preadolescents and Adolescents." Unpublished doctoral dissertation, University of Minnesota, 1999.

Abecassis, M., and others. "Mutual Antipathies and Their Developmental Significance in Middle Childhood and Adolescence." *Child Development*, 2002, *73*, 1543–1556.

Beck, A. T. *Prisoners of Hate: The Cognitive Basis of Anger, Hostility and Violence.* New York: HarperCollins, 1999.

Berndt, T., and Perry, B. "Children's Perceptions of Relationships as Supportive Networks." *Developmental Psychology*, 1986, *22*, 640–648.

Bernicot, J., and Mahrokhian, A. "Asking and Insisting After a Refusal: How Do Six- to Seven-Year-Olds Proceed?" *International Journal of Psychology*, 1989, *24*, 409–428.

Bigelow, B. "Children's Friendship Expectations: A Cognitive Developmental Study." *Child Development*, 1977, *48*, 246–253.

Blumberg, H. "On Being Liked More Than You Like." *Journal of Personality and Social Psychology*, 1969, *11*, 121–128.

Boyer, L. "On Man's Need to Have Enemies: A Psychoanalytic Perspective." *Journal of Psychoanalytic Anthropology*, 1986, *9*, 101–120.

Crick, N. "Relational Aggression: The Role of Intent, Attributions, Feelings of Distress, and Provocation Type." *Development and Psychopathology*, 1995, *7*, 313–322.

Crick, N., and Dodge, K. "A Review and Reformulation of Social Information Processing Mechanisms in Children's Social Adjustment." *Psychological Bulletin*, 1994, *115*, 74–101.

Crick, N., and Dodge, K. "Social Information Processing in Reactive and Proactive Aggression." *Child Development*, 1996, *67*, 993–1002.

Curtis, R., and Miller, K. "Believing Another Likes or Dislikes You: Behaviors Making the Beliefs Come True." *Journal of Personality and Social Psychology*, 1986, *51*, 284–290.

Dodge, K. "Behavioral Antecedents of Peer Social Status." *Child Development*, 1983, *54*, 1386–1399.

Harter, S. "Cognitive-Developmental Process in the Integration of Concepts About Emotion and the Self." *Social Cognition*, 1990, *4*, 119–151.

Hartup, W. W. "The Company They Keep: Friendships and Their Developmental Significance." *Child Development*, 1996, *67*, 1–13.

Hartup, W. W., and Abecassis, M. "Friends and Enemies." In P. Smith and C. Hart (eds.), *Blackwell's Handbook of Social Development.* Cambridge, Mass.: Blackwell, 2002.

Hartup, W. W., Laursen B., Stewart, M., and Eastenson, A. "Conflict and Friendship Relations of Young Children." *Child Development*, 1988, *59*, 1590–1600.

Hayes, D., Gershman, E., and Bolin, L. "Friends and Enemies: Cognitive Bases for Preschool Children's Unilateral and Reciprocal Relationships." *Child Development*, 1980, *51*, 1276–1279.

Hembree, S., and Vandell, D. "Reciprocity in Rejection: The Role of Mutual Antipathy in Predicting Children's Adjustment." Unpublished manuscript, 1999.

Hesse, P., and Mack, J. "The World Is a Dangerous Place: Images of the Enemy on Children's Television." In R. Rieber (ed.), *The Psychology of War and Peace: The Image of the Enemy.* New York: Plenum, 1991.

Higgins, E. "Self Discrepancy: A Theory Relating Self and Affect." *Psychological Review*, 1987, *94*, 319–340.

Holt, R. "College Students' Definitions and Images of Enemies." *Journal of Social Issues*, 1989, *45*, 33–50.

MacDonald, C., and Cohen, R. "Children's Awareness of Which Peers Like Them and Which Peers Dislike Them." *Social Development*, 1995, *4*, 182–193.

Middents, G. "Psychological Perspectives on Enemy Making." *Organization Development Journal*, 1994, *4*, 44–47.

Purdie, V., and Downey, G. "Rejection Sensitivity and Adolescent Girls' Vulnerability to Relationship Centered Difficulties." *Child Maltreatment*, 2000, *5*, 338–350.

Ray, G., and Cohen, R. "Children's Evaluations of Provocation Between Peers." *Aggressive Behavior*, 1997, *23*, 417–431.

Ray, G., and Cohen, R. "Children's Evaluation of Peer Group Entry and Limited Resource Situations." *Merrill Palmer Quarterly,* 2000, *46,* 71–89.

Rieber, R., and Kelly, R. "Substance and Shadow: Images of the Enemy." In R. Rieber (ed.), *The Psychology of War and Peace: The Image of the Enemy.* New York: Plenum, 1991.

Rule, B., Bisanz, G., and Kohn, M. "Anatomy of a Persuasion Schema: Targets, Goals and Strategies." *Journal of Personality and Social Psychology,* 1985, *48,* 1127–1140.

Shallit, B. *The Psychology of Conflict and Combat.* New York: Praeger, 1988.

Sherif, M., and others. *Intergroup Conflict and Cooperation: The Robber's Cave Experiment.* Norman: University of Oklahoma Book Exchange, 1961.

Tesser, A., Campbell, J., and Smith, M., "Friendship Choice and Performance: Self-Evaluation Maintenance in Children." *Journal of Personality and Social Psychology,* 1984, *46,* 561–574.

Volkan, V. "The Need to Have Enemies and Allies: A Developmental Approach." *Political Psychology,* 1985, *6,* 219–247.

Wiseman J., and Duck, S. "Having Enemies and Managing Enemies: A Very Challenging Relationship." In S. Duck and J. Wood (eds.), *Confronting Relationship Challenges.* Thousand Oaks, Calif.: Sage, 1995.

MAURISSA ABECASSIS is assistant professor of psychology and child development at Colby-Sawyer College in New London, New Hampshire.

2

This chapter examines linkages between parenting and peer enemy relationships and looks at the relations between attachment styles and enemy relationships among middle school children.

Parent-Child Relationships and Enmity with Peers: The Role of Avoidant and Preoccupied Attachment

Noel A. Card, Ernest V. E. Hodges

If we are to explore children's and adolescents' inimical relationships with peers, it is necessary to consider possible linkages with the home environment. Parenting and attachment security have repeatedly been shown to be associated with peer relations in terms of both sociometric status and friendships. Connections between aspects of the family context and enemy relationships with peers have not yet been explored. This chapter explores linkages between parent-child relationships and enmity with peers and presents data regarding the relation of avoidant and preoccupied attachment to enemy relationships.

Several aspects of parents and their behavior may have an impact on children's relations with peers. Putallaz and Heflin (1990) outlined the roles of parents' psychological health, interpersonal functioning, warmth, control, and disciplinary practices in predicting children's rejection by peers. According to these authors, characteristics of the parents (aggressiveness, altruism, parental communication), parenting behaviors (sensitivity, warmth, supportiveness, accessibility), and disciplinary techniques (power assertion, love withdrawal, induction) influence children's social behavior with peers through processes of modeling, reinforcement, and response evocation. These social behaviors in turn are related to children's acceptance and rejection by their peer group (Coie, Dodge, and

We thank David G. Perry for commenting on a draft of this chapter.

NEW DIRECTIONS FOR CHILD AND ADOLESCENT DEVELOPMENT, no. 102, Winter 2003 © Wiley Periodicals, Inc.

Kupersmidt, 1990; Newcomb, Bukowski, and Pattee, 1993), suggesting that parents may influence their children's peer relations through processes mediated by the child's social behavior. Parents may also affect their children's group-level status by influencing their children's social motivation, cognitive control, and emotional regulation abilities (Putallaz and Heflin, 1990; see also Parke and Buriel, 1998; Rubin, Bukowski, and Parker, 1998). Other modes of influence that parents may exert on their children's group-level status include direct facilitation, coaching, and monitoring of the children's peer interactions (Ladd, Profilet, and Hart, 1992; Rubin, Bukowski, and Parker, 1998).

There is evidence suggesting that parenting is related to children's positive dyadic relationships, or friendships. Similar to processes by which parents affect the child's group status (influencing social behavior, social motivation, and cognitive control through modeling, reinforcement, and response evocation), the characteristics of parents, parenting behaviors, and disciplinary techniques are associated with the quantity and quality of children's friendships (Doyle and Markiewicz, 1996). However, the dyadic nature of much of parenting, in that it occurs between the child and the parent, suggests that parenting may be especially relevant to childhood friendships (Doyle and Markiewicz, 1996; Sroufe and Fleeson, 1986). Examination of childhood friendships also differs from the study of group-level acceptance and rejection in that it is necessary to consider not only the quantity of children's friendships, but also the characteristics of those friends and qualitative features of the friendships.

Attachment Security and Peer Relations

In examining the role of parenting in children's enemy relationships, one useful starting point may be with parent-child relationships, specifically children's attachments with their mother and father. Parental characteristics (such as psychopathology) and behaviors (such as warmth, responsiveness) are theoretically and empirically linked to children's attachment quality (Ainsworth, 1979; Belsky, 1999; Goldsmith and Alansky, 1987; Thompson, 1998, 1999; van IJzendoorn and De Wolff, 1997). Moreover, there exists a sizable body of literature suggesting the importance of attachment security in children's peer relations (Rubin, Bukowski, and Parker, 1998; Schneider, Atkinson, and Tardif, 2001).

Attachment theory posits that infants are predisposed to form emotional ties with their caregivers—this predisposition being evolutionarily adaptive in promoting a balance of exploration and proximity to the caregiver. It is also evolutionarily adaptive, however, for the nature of this attachment bond to vary depending on the behavior of the caregiver. A history of warm and consistent parenting is related to "secure" (that is, Type B) attachment, which is characterized by the child's use of the attachment figure as a secure base from which to explore, appropriate distress during separation from the caregiver, and age-appropriate affective engagement with the attachment figure. This pattern is in contrast to two forms of insecure attachment classifications: Type A (avoidant, dismissing) attachment, which is associated with parental negativity and rejection, is characterized by limited affective engagement with, avoidance of, and failure to seek comfort from the attachment figure; and Type C attachment (preoccupied, resistant, ambivalent), which is related to inconsistent parenting, is characterized by a need for the attachment figure that impedes independence, difficulty separating from the attachment figure, and difficulty in deriving comfort from the attachment figure when distressed (Ainsworth, Blehar, Waters, and Wall, 1978).

Like other aspects of parenting, attachment security is related to a variety of behavioral, motivational, and regulatory social skills that may have an impact on peer relations (Thompson, 1998, 1999). Attachment theorists have particularly stressed that links between quality of attachment with parents and relationships with peers are accounted for in large part by the internal working models (IWMs) underlying attachment styles (Main, Kaplan, and Cassidy, 1985; Thompson, 1998, 1999). These IWMs of self and relationships not only guide behavior during interactions with peers, but also influence the perceptions of one's own and partners' behavior during interactions. Thus, attachment styles with parents, and the IWMs associated with these styles, may be self-perpetuating in interactions with peers through the elicitation and biased perception of behaviors from the partner. Indeed, evidence suggests that securely attached children, relative to those with insecure parental attachments, are more accepted and less rejected by the peer group (Elicker, Englund, and Sroufe, 1992; Kerns, Klepac, and Cole, 1996). Attachment security also appears to be related to dyadic peer relationships: securely attached children have more friends and have more harmonious, more satisfying, and less conflictual friendships than insecurely attached children (Kerns, 1994; Kerns, Klepac, and Cole, 1996; Park and Waters, 1989).

Until recently, there existed few adequate measures of attachment quality during middle childhood (Kerns, Tomich, Aspelmeier, and Contreras, 2000). This is unfortunate, given that the middle childhood and early adolescence years may be an optimal time to study linkages in parent-child attachment and peer relations. Children at this age still rely heavily on their parents yet spend an increasing amount of time with peers and place increased importance on their relationships with peers (see Rubin, Bukowski, and Parker, 1998). A small number of attachment-based measures have recently been developed, and a recent study demonstrated that all are modestly intercorrelated with each other when administered to nine to twelve year olds (Kerns, Tomich, Aspelmeier, and Contreras, 2000). Although each of these measures has some advantages over the others, an instrument used by Hodges, Finnegan, and Perry (1999) has two major advantages: it yields separate assessments of the child's relationship with mother and with father, and it assesses two distinct dimensions of insecure attachment, avoidance, and preoccupation. The first feature, differential assessment of attachment to mother and father, is advantageous because attachment qualities with these figures show only small to moderate inter-correlations (Fox, Kimmerly, and Schafer, 1991; van IJzendoorn and De Wolff, 1997). The second feature allows tests of the specific-linkage hypothesis (see Finnegan, Hodges, and Perry, 1996). It was noted earlier that secure attachment is generally related to positive behavioral and social outcomes, whereas insecure attachment is often related to negative outcomes. However, these results are often based on pooling together these two forms of insecure attachment. The specific-linkage hypothesis specifies that distinct behavioral and interpersonal difficulties arise from avoidant and preoccupied stances. Support for this hypothesis comes from concurrent and longitudinal studies in which avoidant and preoccupied attachment differentially predict externalizing behaviors, such as aggression and disruptiveness, and internalizing behaviors, such as depression, anxiety, and social withdrawal, respectively (Finnegan, Hodges, and Perry, 1996; Hodges, Finnegan, and Perry, 1999). These externalizing and internalizing behaviors are in turn each related to poor peer relations (Rubin, Bukowski, and Parker, 1998). Thus, although both avoidant and preoccupied attachment styles may contribute to poor peer relations, there appear to exist two distinct routes for children with avoidant versus preoccupied attachment.

Rationale of the Current Study

There are reasons to expect that insecurely attached children will be more likely to have or will have a greater number of enemy relationships. Insecurely attached children, relative to securely attached children, may expect, may consciously or unconsciously elicit, or may simply have social skills deficits that foster inharmonious, aversive interactions with peers. In addition, consistent with the specific-linkage hypothesis, it might be expected that avoidant and preoccupied children traverse different pathways in forming enemies. Avoidant children may form inimical relationships as a result of their higher levels of externalizing behaviors, whereas preoccupied children may form enemies due to their elevated levels of internalizing distress. Both types of these behavioral problems have been demonstrated to be associated with peer enmity (see Abecassis and others, 2002; Chapters Three through Five, this volume). Thus, we will also examine whether externalizing and internalizing behaviors are related to number of enemies and, if so, whether these behaviors fully or partially mediate any associations between attachment styles and number of enemies.

Because enemy relationships are dyadic phenomena, we felt it was important to study not only the number of enemies children have but also the characteristics of those enemies. The formulation of these hypotheses is based on previous research with positive dyads: friends tend to be similar to each other in their avoidance and preoccupation (Hodges, Finnegan, and Perry, 1999). One explanation of this similarity among friends is that befriending peers with similar relationship stances provides acceptance and reinforcement of preexisting relationship stances, resulting in more harmonious interactions. In contrast, it might be expected that interactions of those with dissimilar relationship stances would be unrewarding, as these peers do not provide affirmation for the child's preexisting style of relating to others. Moreover, relationship stance incompatibility is likely aversive, as children with preoccupied styles may be viewed as intrusive and bothersome by children with avoidant styles, and children with avoidant styles may be viewed as unsupportive and rejecting by children with preoccupied styles. Thus, we hypothesized that children would form enemy relationships with those who are both dissimilar in avoidance and preoccupation and incompatible in relationship stances, such that children who are high in one relationship stance will form enmities with peers high in the other relationship stance.

Methods

Participants were 194 children (95 boys, 99 girls; mean age, 12.2 years) in the fourth through eighth grades of a university school serving a primarily middle-class, predominantly white community. All participants had received parental consent, constituting 80 percent of the total population of children in these grades.

Two to three months before the end of the school year, children responded to several instruments administered in their homerooms. Four instruments were used for this study: two instruments assessing children's attachment stances with their mother and father, a peer nomination inventory, and a sociometric instrument.

Attachment Stance Questionnaires. Two self-report questionnaires were administered to assess children's attachment stances with their mothers and fathers. Each instrument consisted of fifteen items assessing avoidant coping styles and fifteen items assessing preoccupied coping styles with the appropriate figure in attachment-relevant stressful situations (for example, separations, novelty; see Hodges, Finnegan, and Perry, 1999). As reported in Hodges, Finnegan, and Perry (1999), these scales were internally consistent and exhibited both convergent and external validity.

Peer Nomination Inventory. Children were asked to nominate an unlimited number of same-sex grademates who manifest a variety of behaviors: aggression (seven items), anxiety-depression (two items), argumentativeness (two items), dishonesty (two items), disruptiveness (two items), hovering peer entry style (one item), prosocial behavior (two items), and withdrawal (two items). A score on each scale was determined by calculating the percentage of same-sex grademates who nominated the child on each item of the scale and then averaging these percentages across scales.

These scales were then standardized by grade and gender. Factor analysis of these scales yielded two factors: Externalizing Problems (aggression, argumentativeness, dishonesty, disruptiveness, and prosocial behavior [negatively loaded]) and Internalizing Problems (anxiety-depression, hovering peer entry style, and withdrawal; see Hodges and Perry, 1999).

Sociometric Instrument. Children were asked to indicate three peers with whom they most like to work or play, as well as three peers with whom they least like to work or play, from a list of participating same-sex grademates (ranging from 14 to 23 peers; $M = 18.4$). A child's enemies were defined as peers who reciprocated the child's nomination of disliking; thus, the number of enemies could range from none to three. The coping styles and behavioral characteristics of each child's enemies were computed by averaging the child's enemies' scores on each relationship stance variable (avoidant and preoccupied coping with mother and father) and on peer-reported externalizing and internalizing problems.

Associations Between Relationship Stances, Behaviors, and Number of Enemies

Based on reciprocated dislike nominations, ninety-four participants (48 percent) had at least one enemy. Fifty-five children (28.4 percent) had one enemy, thirty (15.5 percent) had two enemies, and nine (4.6 percent) had three enemies. There were no significant differences between boys and girls in either presence of at least one enemy (a dichotomous variable) or number of enemies.

Correlations among number of enemies, children's avoidant and preoccupied attachment with their mother and father, and externalizing and internalizing behaviors are displayed in Table 2.1 (standardized by grade and gender). As can be seen in the first row, only one of the four correlations between number of enemies and attachment to parents was significant: number of enemies was related to avoidant stance with father ($r = .16$, $p < .05$). This pattern was similar for both boys and girls, and gender did not significantly moderate the relationship between number of enemies and any of these four attachment measures. These results suggest that the quantity of children's enemies is generally unrelated (or only weakly related) to avoidant or preoccupied attachment to parents.

Although children's relationship stances with their mothers and fathers were generally unrelated to number of enemies, it should be noted that both externalizing and internalizing behaviors were associated with number of inimical relationships. In addition, the initial criteria to evaluate behavioral mediation (Baron and Kenny, 1986) were met for father avoidance and number of enemies. Further analysis indicated that father avoidance failed to significantly predict number of enemies once externalizing was controlled, and externalizing behaviors accounted for 69.2 percent of the association between father avoidance and number of enemies. Thus, it appears

Table 2.1. Intercorrelations Among Variables in the Study

	2	3	4	5	6	7
1. Number of enemies	.07	.10	.16*	.08	.36**	.33**
2. Avoidance with mother		−.38**	.59**	−.29**	.15*	−.13
3. Preoccupied with mother			−.25**	.77**	−.03	.14*
4. Avoidance with father				−.29**	.21**	−.08
5. Preoccupied with father					−.06	.18*
6. Externalizing problems						.03
7. Internalizing problems						

Note: N = 194. *p < .05. **p < .01.

that there is little support for any direct effect of insecure attachment on quantity of enemies. However, the limited support for concurrent behavioral mediation does not preclude the possibility that these processes are in operation over time. That these avoidant and preoccupied stances have been shown to contribute to increases in externalizing and internalizing behaviors (see Hodges, Finnegan, and Perry, 1999) leaves open the possibility that attachment styles play a more distal role in the formation of numerous enmities in the peer group that may be detectable only through longitudinal studies. Alternatively, both attachment quality and number of inimical relationships may antecede externalizing and internalizing behaviors, and relationship stances with parents may thus play little role in predicting the number of enemies children will have in the peer group. Clearly, longitudinal studies evaluating these alternative processes are needed.

Dissimilarity and Incompatibility of Enemies' Relationship Stances

In addition to examining the associations between relationship stances and the quantity of enemies, it may be useful to examine how these relationship stances are related to the characteristics of children's enemies. As noted, we hypothesized that children would form inimical relationships with peers who are dissimilar and incompatible in relationship stances. Table 2.2 shows the correlations between children's avoidant and preoccupied attachment with mother and father with those of their enemies for the ninety-four children with at least one reciprocated enemy. Examination of these correlations shows that children's avoidant attachment with their mother was negatively related to their enemies' avoidant attachment with their mother ($r = -.38$, $p < .01$) and that children's avoidant attachment with their father was marginally negatively related to their enemies' avoidant attachment with father ($r = -.17$, $p < .10$). Similarly, children's preoccupied attachment with their mother was negatively related to their enemies' preoccupied attachment with mother ($r = -.42$, $p < .01$), and children's preoccupied attachment with their father was negatively related to their enemies' preoccupied attachment with father ($r = -.33$, $p < .01$). In general, these relationships did not differ by gender, with the exception of avoidant attachment with father [$F(1,90) = 3.96$, $p < .05$], for which there was a greater degree of dissimilarity among boys' enemy dyads ($r = -.34$, $p < .05$) than among girls' enmities ($r = .04$, ns). These results generally support the hypothesis that enemies are dissimilar in their attachment orientations with their mother and father.

Further examination of Table 2.2 reveals positive correlations between opposite relationship stances, such that children's avoidant stances with their mother and father were positively related to their enemies' preoccupied stances with their mother and father ($r = .44$, $p < .01$ and $r = .25$, $p < .05$, respectively). As is expected given the dyadic nature of these data, relationships between children's preoccupied stances and their enemies' avoidant stances are nearly identical to these results. These findings support the hypothesis that children have enemies with incompatible relationship stances.

Because children's avoidant and preoccupied stances were moderately negatively related ($r = -.38$, $p < .01$ and $r = -.29$, $p < .01$ for attachment to mother and father, respectively), avoidant and preoccupied stances were simultaneously entered into multiple regressions in order to determine whether dissimilarity and incompatibility in relationship stance independently predicted each of the four relationship stances of children's enemies. Children's preoccupied and avoidant attachment with their mother independently predicted their enemies' avoidance with mother (beta = .33, $p < .01$ and beta = $-.22$, $p < .05$, respectively), and children's avoidant and preoccupied attachment with their mother independently predicted their enemies' preoccupation with mother (beta = .31, $p < .01$ and beta = $-.27$, $p < .05$). However, only children's preoccupied attachment with their father independently predicted their enemies' avoidance (beta = -19, $p < .10$) and preoccupation (beta = $-.27$, $p < .05$) with their father. Children's avoidant attachment did not predict either of their enemies' relationship stances

Table 2.2. Associations Between Children's and Enemies' Relationship Stances

Children's Stance	Enemies' Avoidant Stance with Mother	Enemies' Preoccupied Stance with Mother	Enemies' Avoidant Stance with Father	Enemies' Preoccupied Stance with Father
Avoidant stance with mother	$-.38^{**}$	$.44^{**}$	$-.26^{**}$	$.40^{**}$
Preoccupied stance with mother	$.44^{**}$	$-.42^{**}$	$.17\dagger$	$-.38^{**}$
Avoidant stance with father	$-.26^{*}$	$.20^{*}$	$-.17\dagger$	$.25^{*}$
Preoccupied stance with father	$.36^{**}$	$-.35^{**}$	$.23^{*}$	$-.33^{**}$

Note: $N = 94$, $\dagger p < .10$. $^{*}p < .05$. $^{**}p < .01$.

when controlling for preoccupation with father. Taken together, these results generally support the hypothesis that both dissimilarity and incompatibility independently contribute to children's inimical relationships.

Do Behaviors Associated with Relationship Stances Account for Enemy Dissimilarity and Incompatibility?

Further examination of Table 2.1 reveals associations between relationship stances and externalizing and internalizing problems. Specifically, avoidant stances with mother and father are related to externalizing problems ($r = .15$, $p < .05$ and $r = .21$, $p < .01$, respectively), whereas preoccupied stances with mother and father are related to internalizing problems ($r = .14$, $p < .05$; $r = .18$, $p < .01$; Hodges, Finnegan, and Perry, 1999). Thus, it might be expected that the dissimilarity and incompatibility in relationship stances observed within enemy dyads are accounted for by dissimilarity and incompatibility in these overt externalizing and internalizing behaviors. In order to test this possibility, four hierarchical multiple regressions were performed in which each of the enemies' relationship stances served as the dependent variables. To account for dissimilarity and incompatibility in enemies' behaviors, children's internalizing and externalizing problems and their enemies' internalizing and externalizing problems were entered at step 1. At step 2, children's avoidant and preoccupied stances were entered to examine whether they contributed unique variance in predicting the relationship stance of children's enemies above and beyond that accounted for by the overt externalizing and internalizing behaviors of children and their enemies. As can be seen in Table 2.3, children's relationship

Table 2.3. Predicting Enemies' Relationship Stances from Children's Relationship Stances and Overt Externalizing and Internalizing Behaviors

Criterion Variable	Step 1[a] R^2	ΔR^2		β		β
				Step 2		
Enemies' avoidance with mother	.108*	.183**	Avoidance with mother	−.20†	Preoccupation with mother	.32**
Enemies' preoccupation with mother	.096†	.197**	Avoidance with mother	.30**	Preoccupation with mother	−.25*
Enemies' avoidance with father	.127*	.029	Avoidance with father	−.08	Preoccupation with father	.13
Enemies' preoccupation with father	.127*	.078*	Avoidance with father	.11	Preoccupation with father	−.23*

Note: $N = 94$. †$p < .10$. *$p < .05$. **$p < .01$.

[a]At step 1, children's externalizing and internalizing problems and their enemies' externalizing and internalizing were entered.

stances predicted their enemies' relationship stances in three of four analyses, even after controlling for overt behaviors. Thus, it appears that the dissimilarity and incompatibility of enemies' relationship stances are not entirely accounted for by their overt behaviors.

Implications of Findings

Several conclusions and directions for future research are suggested by these findings. First, these results suggest the importance of conceptualizing enemy relationships as dyadic phenomena. This conceptualization suggests future directions for research and theory in illuminating linkages between enemy dyads and other dyadic peer relationships. Second, these results demonstrate that linkages between the family context and peer enmity exist and can be detected, suggesting multiple lines for future research.

Enemy Relationships as Dyadic Phenomena. Although children's avoidant or preoccupied attachment with their mothers and fathers was generally unrelated to the number of enemies children have, these relationship stances were related to the characteristics of children's enemies, such that enemy dyads were marked by both dissimilarity and incompatibility in their relationship stances. These findings highlight the importance of examining enmity as a dyadic phenomenon: the characteristics that result in one child's disliking and being disliked by another peer may differ depending on who that peer is. In other words, enemy dyads differ from unilateral disliking (peer rejection) in that each member of the dyad appears to hold a personalized dislike for the other member and is disliked in an equally personalized manner (Hartup and Abecassis, 2002).

The source of this personalized dislike is likely a result of the behaviors and perceptions of both individuals: the relationship stance of child A is considered especially aversive to child B, and the relationship stance of child B is considered especially aversive to child A. That analyses controlling for overt externalizing and internalizing behaviors suggested that this dissimilarity and incompatibility in attachment was not due simply to overt behaviors associated with these stances supports the claim that perceptions associated with these attachment orientations play an independent role in enemy relationships. (For further discussion of the biased perceptions that may exist within inimical relationships, see Chapter Four, this volume.)

Overlap Between Enmity and Other Dyadic Relationships. Although there were substantial correlations between children's relationship stances and those of their enemies, it is important to point out that there exists variability in the degree to which enemies are dissimilar and incompatible in their attachment. In other words, although many enemy dyads are marked by dissimilarity and incompatibility in relationship stances, some are not. This concept of variability in attachment dissimilarity and incompatibility is important if we are to think of overlap with other dyadic relationships.

One type of negative dyadic relationship that has received attention in terms of attachment styles of its members is the aggressor-victim relationship, which often consists of an avoidant child (the aggressor) and a preoccupied child (the victim; Finnegan, Hodges, and Perry, 1996; Troy and Sroufe, 1987). Thus, it might be expected that enemy dyads consisting of members who are highly dissimilar and incompatible in their attachment styles may be more likely to take the form of an aggressor-victim relationship than enemy dyads whose members are less dissimilar or incompatible. However, the current findings may also provide clues to the manner by which avoidant and preoccupied children enter aggressor-victim relationships. Perhaps this relationship of abuse is preceded by the emergence of enmity between the two peers. Children do exhibit hostile attributional biases of their enemies compared with other peers (Ray and Cohen, 1997), and reports of victimization are more common in enemy relationships compared to those with other peers (Card and Hodges, 2002), suggesting substantial overlap between inimical relationships and aggressor-victim relationships. It must be remembered, however, that not all aggressor-victim relationships are marked by enmity (see Troy and Sroufe, 1987), and it is likely that not all enemy relationships are marked by aggression. Future work is needed to evaluate the degree of overlap between these two types of relationships, as well as the temporal association between them.

Consideration of the relations between friendship and enmity is also needed. A substantial proportion of enemy relationships arise from broken friendships (Card and others, 2002). Given that friends are often similar in their attachment styles (Hodges, Finnegan, and Perry, 1999), those enmities having similar relationship stances may represent a subgroup that were formerly friends but could not successfully manage conflict or jealousy that arose within that friendship. Alternatively, friends who are most dissimilar and incompatible in their attachment may be most likely to transform into enemies, and these enemies may not differ from others (for example, aggressor-victim enemies) in their attachment dissimilarity and incompatibility. Also, some enemies may eventually reconcile and become friends— perhaps those who are least dissimilar and incompatible in their attachment styles. Again, further research is needed examining the temporal relation between these two types of relationships and the role that attachment styles may play in these transformations.

Linkages Between the Family Context and Enemy Relationships with Peers. Although previous research has demonstrated linkages between the home context and relations with peers in terms of group-level acceptance and rejection and in terms of friendships, this is the first study to explore associations between the home context and children's enemy relationships. The findings illustrate linkages between children's attachment with their parents and enemy relationships with peers. However, we stated earlier that a useful beginning step in exploring the relations between parenting and childhood enmity might be examination of attachment styles. This should not be the last step. Although attachment security captures many aspects of the family environment, it fails to capture a range of methods by which parents influence their children's peer relations. Indeed, associations between parenting behaviors and attachment styles, while significant, are generally not strong (Goldsmith and Alansky, 1987; van IJzendoorn and De Wolff, 1997). Thus, it may behoove researchers to explore the specific aspects of parenting that are related to childhood enmity. For example, parents may directly teach (through modeling, reinforcement, and coaching) their children social skills and conflict management strategies not reflected by attachment security, which may nevertheless be relevant to enemy relationships with peers.

Other aspects of parenting may be more directly linked to children's enmity. Do parents model behavior and attributions toward enemies through their interactions with and conversations about their own enemies? Do parents coach children on how to deal with inimical relationships? If so, how, and what methods are most effective? Direct measures of parenting behaviors in general, and parenting specific to enmity, are desirable in the future study of children's enemy relationships.

Limitations and Future Directions. Several limitations of this research merit attention. Most notable is the use of a concurrent correlational design. Although we have conceptualized the dissimilarity and incompatibility of attachment styles as important in the formation of enemy relationships, it may also be possible that enemy relationships affect children's relationship stances with their mothers and fathers, perhaps by entrenching preexisting stances. Longitudinal research is necessary to determine whether attachment orientations antecede enemy relationships and if enmities account for changes in relationship stances over time. Longitudinal research would also allow for the examination of whether dissimilarity and incompatibility in attachment are related to the stability of enemy relationships (see Chapter Five, this volume).

Another limitation of this study is the failure to assess behavioral interactions occurring within the enemy dyads. This limitation is relevant in two ways. First, peer-reported externalizing and internalizing behaviors were used to test whether overt behaviors could account for the dissimilarity and incompatibility of enemies' relationship stances. However, it is unclear to what degree peer nominations of these behaviors capture the behaviors occurring in interactions between enemies. Thus, it may be premature to conclude that children's interpersonal behaviors do not account for the dissimilarity and incompatibility of enemies. Our measures of externalizing and internalizing behaviors may simply not have captured the behaviors occurring within these enemy relationships. Second, if we are to understand enemy relationships and what they entail, it is necessary to have a fuller understanding of the interactions occurring between enemies. Past research has offered a rich understanding of how friends interact (Hartup, 1989; Hartup and Abecassis, 2002; Newcomb and Bagwell, 1995), yet we have little knowledge about enemies. Although the other chapters in this volume provide some knowledge, observational studies of enemies' interactions are needed. The links between the home environment and these interactions remain a fruitful avenue for future research.

This study's focus on attachment styles represents only one of many aspects of parenting that could be examined. Although further examination of other aspects of parenting is needed, future research should not limit itself to the study of parenting. Instead, a wider range of distal factors potentially related to childhood enmity should be considered. How systemic features of the family environment (such as spousal and sibling relationships), social aspects of the family (parents' relationships with other adults and parents' and siblings' relationships with parents and siblings of peers, for example), and the wider context in which the family operates (neighborhood characteristics, cultural factors; see Chapter Three, this volume) are related to childhood enmity are currently unknown questions worthy of future exploration.

References

Abecassis, M., and others. "Mutual Antipathies and Their Significance in Middle Childhood and Adolescence." *Child Development,* 2002, *73,* 1543–1556.

Ainsworth, M.D.S. "Infant-Mother Attachment." *American Psychologist,* 1979, *34,* 932–937.

Ainsworth, M.D.S., Blehar, M. C., Waters, E., and Wall, S. *Patterns of Attachment: A Psychological Study of the Strange Situation.* Mahwah, N.J.: Erlbaum, 1978.

Baron, R. M., and Kenny, D. A. "The Moderator-Mediator Variable Distinction in Social Psychological Research: Conceptual, Strategic, and Statistical Considerations." *Journal of Personality and Social Psychology,* 1986, *51,* 1173–1182.

Belsky, J. "Interactional and Contextual Determinants of Attachment Security." In J. Cassidy and P. R. Shaver (eds.), *Handbook of Attachment.* New York: Guilford Press, 1999.

Card, N. A., and others. "Enemy Relationships in Adolescence: Formation, Maintenance, Impact, and Typologies." Poster presented at the seventeenth biennial meeting of the International Society for the Study of Behavioural Development, Ottawa City, Ottawa, 2002.

Card, N. A., and Hodges, E.V.E. "The Danger of Enemies: Implications of Dyadic Mutual Animosity for Victimization by Peers." Unpublished manuscript, St. John's University, 2002.

Coie, J. D., Dodge, K. A., and Kupersmidt, J. B. "Peer Group Behavior and Social Status." In S. R. Asher and J. D. Coie (eds.), *Peer Rejection in Childhood.* Cambridge: Cambridge University Press, 1990.

Doyle, A. B., and Markiewicz, D. "Parents' Interpersonal Relationships and Children's Friendships." In W. M. Bukowski, A. F. Newcomb, and W. W. Hartup (eds.), *The Company They Keep: Friendship in Childhood and Adolescence.* Cambridge: Cambridge University Press, 1996.

Elicker, J., Englund, M., and Sroufe, L. A. "Predicting Peer Competence and Peer Relationships in Childhood from Early Parent-Child Relationships." In R. D. Parke and G. W. Ladd (eds.), *Family-Peer Relationships: Models of Linkage.* Mahwah, N.J.: Erlbaum, 1992.

Finnegan, R. A., Hodges, E.V.E., and Perry, D. G. "Preoccupied and Avoidant Coping During Middle Childhood." *Child Development,* 1996, *67,* 1318–1328.

Fox, N. A., Kimmerly, N. L., and Schafer, W. D. "Attachment to Mother/Attachment to Father: A Meta-Analysis." *Child Development*, 1991, 62, 210–225.

Goldsmith, H. H., and Alansky, J. A. "Maternal and Temperamental Predictors of Attachment: A Meta-Analytic Review." *Journal of Consulting and Clinical Psychology*, 1987, 55, 805–816.

Hartup, W. W. "Behavioral Manifestations of Children's Friendships." In T. J. Berndt and G. W. Ladd (eds.), *Peer Relationships in Child Development*. New York: Wiley, 1989.

Hartup, W. W., and Abecassis, M. "Friends and Enemies." In P. K. Smith and C. H. Hart (eds.), *Blackwell Handbook of Childhood Social Development*. Cambridge, Mass.: Blackwell, 2002.

Hodges, E.V.E., Finnegan, R. A., and Perry, D. G. "Skewed Autonomy-Relatedness in Preadolescents' Conceptions of Their Relationships with Mother, Father, and Best Friend." *Developmental Psychology*, 1999, 35, 737–748.

Hodges, E.V.E., and Perry, D. G. "Personal and Interpersonal Antecedents and Consequences of Victimization by Peers." *Journal of Personality and Social Psychology*, 1999, 76, 677–685.

Kerns, K. A. "A Longitudinal Examination of Links Between Mother-Child Attachment and Children's Friendships in Early Childhood." *Journal of Social and Personal Relationships*, 1994, 11, 379–381.

Kerns, K. A., Klepac, L., and Cole, A. K. "Peer Relationships and Preadolescents' Perceptions of Security in the Child-Mother Relationship." *Developmental Psychology*, 1996, 32, 457–466.

Kerns, K. A., Tomich, P. L., Aspelmeier, J. E., and Contreras, J. M. "Attachment-Based Assessments of Parent-Child Relationships in Middle Childhood." *Developmental Psychology*, 2000, 36, 614–626.

Ladd, G. W., Profilet, S., and Hart, C. H. "Parents' Management of Children's Peer Relations: Facilitating and Supervising Children's Activities in the Peer Culture." In R. D. Parke and G. W. Ladd (eds.), *Family-Peer Relationships: Modes of Linkage*. Mahwah, N.J.: Erlbaum, 1992.

Main, M., Kaplan, N., and Cassidy, J. "Security in Infancy, Childhood, and Adulthood: A Move to the Level of Representation." In I. Bretherton and E. Waters (eds.), *Growing Points of Attachment Theory and Research*. Monographs of the Society for Research in Child Development, 50(1–2, Serial no. 209), 1985.

Newcomb, A. F., and Bagwell, C. L. "Children's Friendship Relations: A Meta-Analytic Review." *Psychological Bulletin*, 1995, 117, 306–347.

Newcomb, A. F., Bukowski, W. M., and Pattee, L. "Children's Peer Relations: A Meta-Analytic Review of Popular, Rejected, Neglected, Controversial, and Average Sociometric Status." *Psychological Bulletin*, 1993, 113, 99–128.

Park, K. A., and Waters, E. "Security of Attachment and Preschool Friendships." *Child Development*, 1989, 60, 1076–1081.

Parke, R. D., and Buriel, R. "Socialization in the Family: Ethnic and Ecological Perspectives." In W. Damon (series ed.) and N. Eisenberg (ed.), *Handbook of Child Psychology: Vol. 3, Social, Emotional, and Personality Development*. New York: Wiley, 1998.

Putallaz, M., and Heflin, A. H. "Parent-Child Interaction." In S. R. Asher and J. D. Coie (eds.), *Peer Rejection in Childhood*. Cambridge: Cambridge University Press, 1990.

Ray, G. E., and Cohen, R. "Children's Evaluations of Provocation Between Peers." *Aggressive Behavior*, 1997, 23, 417–431.

Rubin, K. H., Bukowski, W. M., and Parker, J. G. "Peer Interactions, Relationships, and Groups." In W. Damon (series ed.) and N. Eisenberg (ed.), *Handbook of Child Psychology: Vol. 3, Social, Emotional, and Personality Development*. New York: Wiley, 1998.

Schneider, B. H., Atkinson, L., and Tardif, C. "Child-Parent Attachment and Children's Peer Relations: A Quantitative Review." *Developmental Psychology,* 2001, *37,* 86–100.

Sroufe, L. A., and Fleeson, J. "Attachment and the Construction of Relationships." In W. W. Hartup and Z. Rubin (eds.), *Relationships and Development.* Mahwah, N.J.: Erlbaum, 1986.

Thompson, R. A. "Early Sociopersonality Development." In W. Damon (series ed.) and N. Eisenberg (ed.), *Handbook of Child Psychology: Vol. 3, Social, Emotional, and Personality Development.* New York: Wiley, 1998.

Thompson, R. A. "Early Attachment and Later Development." In J. Cassidy and P. R. Shaver (eds.), *Handbook of Attachment.* New York: Guilford Press, 1999.

Troy, M., and Sroufe, L. A. "Victimization Among Preschoolers: Role of Attachment Relationship History." *Journal of the American Academy of Child and Adolescent Psychiatry,* 1987, *26,* 166–172.

van IJzendoorn, M., and De Wolff, M. "In Search of the Absent Father: Meta-Analysis of Infant-Father Attachment." *Child Development,* 1997, *68,* 604–609.

NOEL A. CARD *is a doctoral candidate in clinical psychology at St. John's University, Jamaica, New York.*

ERNEST V. E. HODGES *is an associate professor of psychology at St. John's University, Jamaica, New York.*

3

This chapter focuses on the moderating role of inimical peer relationships in the association between community violence exposure and children's functioning difficulties. A series of hierarchical regression analyses demonstrated that community violence exposure is consistently related to psychosocial maladjustment only for children who are involved in a relatively high number of mutual antipathies with peers.

Mutual Antipathies in the Peer Group as a Moderating Factor in the Association Between Community Violence Exposure and Psychosocial Maladjustment

*David Schwartz, Andrea Hopmeyer-Gorman,
Robin L. Toblin, Tania Abou-ezzeddine*

Although murder and assault rates in the United States have steadily declined over the past decade (Blumstein and Wallman, 2000), many of America's children continue to live in chronically violent neighborhoods. The results of survey investigations suggest that by their elementary school years, most inner-city children have already had firsthand encounters with serious acts of neighborhood violence (Martinez and Richters, 1993; Osofsky, Wewers, Hann, and Fick, 1993). These children appear to be at risk for maladjustment across domains of functioning. Researchers have described moderately strong associations between community violence exposure and internalized distress (Kliewer, Lepore, Oskin, and Johnson, 1998), aggression and other disruptive behaviors (Gorman-Smith and Tolan, 1998), academic difficulties (Overstreet and Braun, 1999), and social problems with peers (Schwartz and Proctor, 2000).

Initially, research on community violence exposure was guided primarily by main-effect models of risk, with linear relations expected between exposure and maladjustment. However, investigators recently have begun to posit interactive models, which hold that the outcomes associated with violence exposure vary systematically as a function of the absence or presence of external mechanisms (Kliewer, Lepore, Oskin, and Johnson, 1998). One

NEW DIRECTIONS FOR CHILD AND ADOLESCENT DEVELOPMENT, no. 102, Winter 2003 © Wiley Periodicals, Inc.

primary focus of these models has been on the buffering influence of social support from peers and family (Hill and Madhere, 1996). In this regard, evidence has begun to emerge that positive social relationships can mitigate the risk associated with urban violence (Richters and Martinez, 1993). These findings are consistent with related research on children's peer relationships, which has focused on the protective influence of dyadic friendships (Hodges, Malone, and Perry, 1997; Hodges, Boivin, Vitaro, and Bukowski, 1999). Investigators have found that the strength of the association between violence exposure (such as domestic violence) and negative outcomes is attenuated for children who are able to establish friendships with peers (Bolger, Patterson, and Kupersmidt, 1998; Schwartz and others, 2000).

This chapter seeks to extend the existing interactive models by focusing on more maladaptive social relationships with peers. Our objective was to investigate the potential moderating role of inimical peer relationships in the association between exposure to violence in the community and psychosocial difficulties. Emerging evidence suggests that children who are involved in high-conflict dyadic relationships in the peer group are likely to be characterized by difficulties modulating anger and other emotional states (Dodge, Price, Coie, and Christopoulos, 1990). These regulatory deficits, and the stress associated with frequent conflict with peers, could exacerbate the adjustment difficulties associated with exposure to neighborhood violence. Accordingly, we hypothesized that dyadic enmities in the peer group would be associated with heightened vulnerability to the pernicious impact of community violence exposure.

While considering the potential role of animosities with peers, we made a careful distinction between rejection by the peer group as a whole and antipathies in the context of specific dyadic relationships (Abecassis and others, 2002). The existing literature on disliking in children's peer groups has generally focused on the determinants and outcomes of rebuff by the peer group (Deater-Deckard, 2001) and only rarely has included a focus on dyadic relationships (Coie and others, 1999; Hubbard and others, 2001). Nonetheless, research on other aspects of children's social functioning with peers (for example, research on the distinction between dyadic friendship and acceptance at the level of the peer group; see Schwartz and others, 2000) has consistently highlighted the unique contributions of both group processes and dyadic relationships to children's development. Thus, there may be distinct patterns of outcomes associated with dyadic enmities and peer group rejection (Chapters Five and Six, this volume).

In our investigation, we assessed disliking at both the group and dyadic levels. We expected that animosities in dyadic relationships would play a particularly significant role in the linkage between community violence exposure and psychosocial maladjustment. As past authors have suggested, mutual antipathies within dyads can involve forms of rejection that are more personal and intense than disliking at the group level (Hartup and Abecassis, 2002). Inimical relationships of this nature are also likely to be indicative of specific factors that could increase risk for maladjustment following community violence exposure. For example, Hubbard and others (2001) found that social information processing biases that are specific to dyadic relationships (that is, tendencies to see the behavior of a particular peer as provocative or hostile) predict aggressive behavior independent of the prediction associated with more global social cognitive deficits.

We focused on adjustment difficulties that have been linked to violence exposure by previous investigators. Specifically, we examined relations between community violence exposure and internalized distress (Martinez and Richters, 1993), aggressive behavior (Gorman-Smith and Tolan, 1998), and academic difficulties (Overstreet and Braun, 1999). Because violence exposure in the community can also have negative implications for children's social adjustment with peers (Schwartz and Proctor, 2000), we conducted additional analyses examining deficits in social skills (withdrawal or nonassertiveness) and bullying by peers. Our hypothesis was that the association between community violence exposure and these difficulties would be relatively strong for children who are frequently involved in mutual antipathies with peers.

In a more descriptive vein, we explored gender differences in the moderating role of mutual antipathies. Relatively little is known about gender differences in the prevalence and correlates of dyadic animosities for boys and girls (Abecassis and others, 2002; Chapter Four, this volume). However, gender has emerged as an important factor in the literature on children living in violent urban neighborhoods. A number of investigators have found that boys, compared to girls, are more likely to be victims and witnesses of community violence (excluding sexual violence; see Bell and Jenkins, 1993). In addition, community violence exposure may be more closely associated with some forms of internalized distress for girls than boys (Fitzpatrick and Boldizar, 1993; Singer, Anglin, Song, and Lunghofer, 1995).

The described research questions were examined in a sample of inner-city elementary school children recruited from neighborhoods with moderately high rates of crime and poverty. We focused on the effects of community violence in middle childhood because individual differences in aggression and other social difficulties tend to stabilize at this developmental stage (Coie and Dodge, 1997). There is also some preliminary evidence that reciprocated animosities between peers are relatively common during middle childhood (Abecassis and others, 2002).

Method

Here we summarize the basic design of this investigation, which was conducted within the context of a larger series of investigations focusing on the social adjustment of children living in violent urban neighborhoods (Schwartz and Hopmeyer-Gorman, 2003).

Participants. All children in sixteen third-, fourth-, and fifth-grade classrooms from an elementary school in an urban section of southern California were invited to take part in the project. Of these children, 80 percent returned parental permission and assented to participate. The classrooms ranged in size from twenty to thirty students, with at least 70 percent of the children in each classroom participating (some consenting children were absent from school during data collection). There were 239 children (119 boys, 120 girls) in the final sample. The ethnic/racial composition of the sample was as follows: 48 percent Hispanic American, 23 percent European American, 13 percent Asian American, 2 percent African American, 4 percent unclassified, and 18 percent other background.

Measures. Our measured strategy is presented next. We adopted a multi-informant approach, with data obtained from self-report questionnaires, peer nominations, and a review of school records.

Violence Exposure. Children completed the Community Experiences Questionnaire (CEQ), a self-report questionnaire that was developed and validated in a previous investigation (Schwartz and Proctor, 2000). The CEQ contains separate subscales assessing exposure to community violence through direct victimization and through witnessing. However, for this investigation, we focused only on direct victimization (11 items; alpha = .85).

Social Rejection and Mutual Antipathies. A peer nomination inventory was group administered to the children. Children were given a copy of a class roster and asked to nominate up to three peers who fit the item, "Kids you like least in the whole class." A social rejection score was then generated from the total number of nominations received by each child, standardized within class.

In addition, children who simultaneously nominated each other as "liked least" were considered to be involved in a mutual antipathy, and the total number of antipathies including each child was calculated (possible range of 0 to 3; $M = .37$, $SD = .66$). Approximately 29 percent of the children were involved in at least one mutual antipathy (22.2 percent with one antipathy, 5.1 percent with two antipathies, 1.7 percent with three antipathies). Boys were somewhat more likely than girls to have a mutual antipathy (34.5 percent for boys; 23.3 percent for girls), although the difference was not statistically significant, $\chi^2(3, N = 239) = 6.95$, ns. Thirty-nine percent of the mutual antipathies involved children of the same gender.

Social Behavior and Adjustment. The peer nomination inventory also featured a series of items describing aspects of children's behavioral and social adjustment. Two descriptors were included for each of the following constructs: aggression ("hits or pushes other kids," "bullies or teases other kids"; $r = .80$, $p < .0001$), bullying by peers ("hit or pushed by other kids," "bullied or teased by other kids"; $r = .69$, $p < .0001$), withdrawal ("likes to play alone," "would rather be alone than be with other kids"; $r = .72$, $p <$

.0001), and assertiveness ("is a good leader," "can stand up for themselves without hitting, fighting, or getting angry"; $r = .67$, $p < .0001$).

Depression. Children completed the Children's Depression Inventory (CDI; Kovacs, 1985). This measure has twenty-seven items requiring children to choose one of three sentences describing varying degrees of severity in symptoms, although we excluded an item that assessed suicidal ideation. A depression score was calculated from the mean of the remaining twenty-six items (alpha = .85).

Academic Functioning. Children's grade point average (GPA) was obtained from a review of school records. We assigned numerical scores to letter grades, ranging from F = 1 to A = 5. GPA was calculated as the mean of the math and reading grades ($r = .65$, $p < .0001$).

Procedure. Data collection began approximately six weeks after the start of the fall semester. All measures were administered to the participating children in a one-hour group testing session, conducted by one of the authors or by a trained research assistant. Standardized instructions were read to the children, and questionnaire items were also read aloud.

Results

Our analytic strategy and results are described next.

Mutual Antipathies and Children's Psychosocial Adjustment. Our primary objective was to examine the moderating influence of mutual antipathies on the adjustment outcomes associated with community violence exposure. However, given the limited availability of descriptive research on disliking in dyadic peer relationships, we began with a series of analyses focusing on the correlates of mutual antipathies. Table 3.1 summarizes bivariate relations among all variables. As shown, there was a moderately strong correlation between mutual antipathies and social rejection. That is, children who were involved in a relatively high number of these reciprocated enmities were also disliked by the peer group as a whole. In addition, the total number of mutual antipathies was positively correlated with community violence exposure, aggression, and social withdrawal.

Next, we examined gender differences in the pattern of bivariate effects. Community violence exposure and each of the five adjustment variables were predicted from gender, mutual antipathies, and the mutual antipathies by gender interaction. There was a significant mutual antipathies by gender interaction in the prediction of aggression (beta = -16, $p < .05$) and a marginal interaction for depression, (beta = $-.13$, $p < .075$). Follow-up analyses indicated that for boys, mutual antipathies was positively correlated with aggression ($r = .38$, $p < .0001$) and depression ($r = .21$, $p < .05$). In contrast, for girls, the total number of mutual antipathies was not correlated with either of these adjustment indicators (for aggression, $r = .08$; for depression, $r = -.07$).

Table 3.1. Bivariate Correlations Among All Variables

Variable	1	2	3	4	5	6	7	8	9	10
1. Community Violence Exposure	—	.24***	.24***	.23***	.15†	.05	−.18*	−.25***	.36***	−.19*
2. Mutual Antipathies		—	.42***	.33***	.21**	.21*	−.14†	−.05	.09	−.16†
3. Social Rejection			—	.65***	.46***	.25***	−.26***	−.23***	.10	−.22***
4. Aggression				—	.37***	.09	−.05	−.27***	.06	−.39***
5. Bullying by Peers					—	.36***	−.17†	−.20*	−.12	−.33***
6. Withdrawal						—	−.12	−.09	.17†	−.04
7. Assertiveness							—	.38***	−.20	−.01
8. Grade Point Average								—	−.30***	.16†
9. Depression									—	−.05
10. Gender										—

Note: Effects are evaluated using a relatively conservative critical value of alpha = .005, in order to minimize inflation of type I error rates. See the text for further details. †$p < .05$ (marginally significant). *$p < .005$. **$p < .001$. ***$p < .0005$.

These findings suggest a modest link between inimical peer relationships and children's psychosocial adjustment. Children who had a relatively large number of mutual antipathies were rejected by the peer group as a whole and were characterized by aggression and social withdrawal. These children also tended to report high levels of community violence exposure. However, the total number of mutual antipathies was not associated with difficulties in any of the other adjustment domains (such as academic functioning) assessed in this study. In addition, the correlations for a subset of the indicators (aggression and depression) were significant only for boys.

Relations Between Mutual Antipathies and Psychosocial Maladjustment Independent of Social Rejection. In the analyses already summarized, we found a moderately strong correlation between mutual antipathies and social rejection. This finding is not surprising given that the two indices of disliking by peers were generated from the same peer nomination item. On a conceptual level, some overlap in children who experience rebuff at the group and dyadic levels might also be expected (Abecassis and others, 2002). Nonetheless, this positive correlation does complicate the interpretation of our findings. Children who are involved in numerous dyadic animosities may experience maladjustment primarily because they are also rejected by the peer group as a whole.

To address this issue, we specified a series of models predicting community violence exposure and each of the five adjustment indicators from gender, mutual antipathies, and social rejection. As Table 3.2 depicts, mutual antipathies and social rejection each had independent associations with community violence exposure (the effect for rejection was marginal). Moreover, social rejection was significantly associated with four of the five maladjustment indicators, although the variance associated with mutual antipathies had been controlled. In contrast, mutual antipathies accounted for only a modest unique increment in the prediction of social withdrawal and was not significantly related to any of the remaining indicators.

These findings provide some evidence that mutual antipathies are associated with child dysfunction primarily because children who are involved in these dyadic enmities also tend to be rejected by the peer group as a whole. Indeed, after we removed the variance predicted by social rejection, the mutual antipathies score was not strongly associated with any of the assessed dimensions of maladjustment. However, it may be important to note that there are differences in the psychometric properties of the two indices (a more restricted range of possible values for the mutual antipathies score) that could have influenced these results.

The Moderating Effect of Mutual Antipathies. We now address our central hypotheses, which focused on the potential moderating role of mutual antipathies. We expected that the association between community violence exposure and children's adjustment difficulties would increase as a function of children's involvement in mutual antipathies with peers. To examine this hypothesis, we conducted a series of hierarchical regression

Table 3.2. Summary of Regression Analyses Predicting Community Violence Exposure and Psychosocial Outcomes from Gender, Mutual Antipathies, and Social Rejection

Variable	Gender		Mutual Antipathies		Social Rejection		Total Variance
	β	sr^2	β	sr^2	β	sr^2	R^2
Community Violence Exposure	−.14	.02*	.16	.02*	.13	.01†	.10***
Aggression	−.26	.06***	.05	.00	.56	.25***	.49***
Bullying by Peers	−.24	.05***	.00	.00	.40	.13***	.26***
Withdrawal	.12	.01†	.15	.02*	.22	.04***	.09***
Assertiveness	−.07	.00	−.03	.00	−.26	.05***	.07***
Depression	−.02	.00	.06	.00	.07	.00	.01
Grade Point Average	.13	.02†	.08	.01	−.24	.04***	.07***

Note: †$p < .075$ (marginally significant). *$p < .05$. **$p < .01$. ***$p < .005$.

analyses. Each of the psychosocial adjustment variables was predicted from the main effects of gender, community violence exposure, and mutual antipathies (step 1); the two-way interactions for community violence exposure by gender, mutual antipathies by gender, and community violence exposure by mutual antipathies (step 2); and the three-way interaction for community violence by mutual antipathies by gender (step 3). Interactions were calculated based on mean-centered scores (according to Aiken and West, 1991). As shown in Table 3.3, these analyses yielded significant community violence exposure by mutual antipathies interactions in the prediction of bullying by peers and aggression. In addition, there were significant community violence exposure by mutual antipathies by gender interactions in the prediction of depression and GPA and a marginal interaction in the prediction of withdrawal.

To explore the nature of these interactions, we conducted a series of follow-up analyses. First, we specified models predicting aggression and bullying by peers from community violence exposure with mutual antipathies fixed at low (1 SD below the mean), medium (mean), and high (1 SD above the mean) levels (Aiken and West, 1991). Consistent with our hypotheses, the slope of the relation between community violence exposure and aggression increased steadily as the level of mutual antipathies moved from low (beta = .05, ns), to medium (beta = .12, $p < .075$), to high (beta = .19, $p < .005$). Similarly, the slope of the relation between community violence exposure and bullying by peers increased as the level of mutual antipathies went from low (beta = .00, ns), to medium (beta = .06, ns), to high (beta = .15, $p < .05$).

Analyses were then conducted to explore the community violence exposure by mutual antipathies by gender interactions for withdrawal, depression, and GPA. Each of these three adjustment indicators was predicted from the main effect of community violence exposure, the main effect

Table 3.3. Analyses of the Moderating Role of Mutual Antipathies in the Association Between Community Violence Exposure and Psychosocial Maladjustment

| | Step 1 | | | | | | | | Step 2 | | | | Step 3 | |
| | Main Effect of Gender | | Main Effect of MA | | Main Effect of CVE | | Gender by MA | | Gender by CVE | | MA by CVE | | MA by CVE by Gender | |
Adjustment Variable	β	sr²	β	sr²	β	sr²	β	sr²	β	sr²	β	sr²	β	sr²
Aggression	−.33	.11***	.25	.06***	.10	.01	−.15	.02*	−.01	.00	.12	.02*	.08	.00
Bullying by Peers	−.30	.08***	.15	.02*	.06	.00	−.10	.01	.04	.00	.15	.02**	−.03	.00
Withdrawal	.09	.01	.22	.04**	.01	.00	.09	.01	−.04	.00	.14	.01	−.16	.02
Assertiveness	−.06	.00	−.12	.01	−.16	.03*	−.04	.00	.07	.00	.07	.00	−.06	.00
Depression	.02	.00	−.01	.00	.36	.12***	−.17	.02*	.06	.00	.08	.00	−.19	.02*
Grade Point Average	.12	.01	.03	.00	−.24	.05***	.04	.00	.11	.01	.03	.01	−.21	.03***

Note: All terms are entered simultaneously at each step, with steps entered sequentially. MA = Mutual Antipathies. CVE = Community Violence Exposure. †*p* < .075 (marginally significant). **p* < .05. ***p* < .01. ****p* < .005.

of mutual antipathies, and the two-way interaction between community violence exposure and mutual antipathies. Separate models were specified by gender.

For boys, there were significant community violence exposure by mutual antipathies interactions in the prediction of withdrawal (beta = .29, $p < .01$) and depression (beta = .22, $p < .05$). The corresponding effects for girls were nonsignificant. There was a significant community violence exposure by mutual antipathies interaction in the prediction of GPA (beta = $-.19$ $p < .05$) for girls, whereas the corresponding effect for boys did not approach significance.

We then specified models predicting withdrawal and depression from community violence exposure, with mutual antipathies fixed at low, medium, and high levels. Only boys were included in these analyses. The association between community violence exposure and depression grew stronger as the level of mutual antipathies increased from low (beta = .13, ns), to medium (beta = .25, $p < .01$), to high (beta = .37, $p < .0001$). A similar pattern held for withdrawal, with the slopes moving in a positive direction as mutual antipathies went from low (beta = $-.21$, $p < .05$), to medium (beta = $-.05$, ns), to high (beta = .10, ns).

Follow-up analyses were also conducted for GPA only for girls. The negative association between community violence exposure and GPA grew stronger as the level of mutual antipathies moved from low (beta = .03, ns), to medium (beta = $-.14$, ns), to high (beta = $-.32$ $p < .005$).

Overall, these findings are quite consistent with our hypotheses. Mutual antipathies in the peer group appeared to exert a moderating influence on the relation between community violence exposure and children's functioning difficulties. Most notably, the association between exposure to violence in the community and children's social maladjustment (as indexed by aggressive behavior and bullying by peers) was significant only at high levels of mutual antipathies. However, differences in the pattern of results across gender groups complicated interpretation of the findings. For boys, mutual antipathies moderated the association between violence exposure in the community and internalizing problems such as depression and withdrawal. For girls, mutual antipathies had a stronger influence on the relation between community violence exposure and academic outcomes.

The Moderating Effect of Social Rejection. We have already described evidence that the pattern of bivariate relations between mutual antipathies and the maladjustment indicators reflects the indirect influence of social rejection (see Table 3.2). Interpretation of the higher-order effects summarized above may be complicated by similar difficulties. That is, mutual antipathies could moderate the link between community violence exposure and children's maladjustment partially because these dyadic enmities tend to be associated with rejection by the full peer group. Analyses that include simultaneous control for interactions between community violence exposure and each form of peer group disliking might help to resolve this issue. Unfortunately, we lacked the statistical power to examine regression models of this complexity.

As an alternative, we focused directly on the moderating role of social rejection. Our goal was to investigate the possibility that social rejection and mutual antipathies have similar implications for children's adjustment following community violence exposure. That is, we sought to determine if rejection by the full peer group increases the strength of the association between violence exposure in the community and functioning difficulties. Each of the psychosocial adjustment variables was predicted from the main effects of gender, community violence exposure, and social rejection (step 1); the two-way interactions for community violence exposure by gender, social rejection by gender, and community violence exposure by social rejection (step 2); and the three-way interaction for community violence exposure by social rejection by gender (step 3). There was a significant two-way community violence exposure by social rejection interaction in the prediction of withdrawal (beta = $-.17$, $p < .05$). However, no other significant two-way or three-way interaction effects emerged.

To decompose the interaction effect for withdrawal, we conducted a series of follow-up analyses. Withdrawal was predicted from community violence exposure with social rejection fixed at low, medium, and high levels (Aiken and West, 1991). The association between community violence exposure and withdrawal moved from a negative to a positive slope as the level of social rejection increased from low (beta = $-.21$, $p < .05$), to medium (beta = $-.06$, ns), to high (beta = $.08$, ns). Interestingly, we did not find a significant positive relation between withdrawal and community violence exposure at any level of social rejection.

The full pattern of results does not support a conceptualization of social rejection as a moderating process. In fact, the relation between community violence exposure and children's maladjustment appeared to be largely unaffected by social rejection. Although rebuff at the level of the full peer group is likely to have a negative impact on children's functioning over time (Parker and Asher, 1987), peer rejection does not seem to exacerbate the adjustment problems associated with violence exposure in the community.

Implications of Our Findings

The findings of this investigation highlight the potential significance of inimical peer relationships for the adjustment of children living in violent urban neighborhoods. Like previous researchers (Kliewer, Lepore, Oskin, and Johnson, 1998; Schwartz and Proctor, 2000), we found a pattern of modest to moderate associations between children's self-reports of community violence exposure and indicators of psychosocial maladjustment. However, mutual antipathies in the peer group appeared to play an important role in these linkages. Exposure to neighborhood violence was consistently related to functioning difficulties only for children who were involved in a relatively high number of these dyadic animosities.

What underlies the moderating influence of mutual antipathies in the peer group? One possibility is that enmities between peers exacerbate the impact of urban violence by facilitating the development of aggression and other externalizing behaviors. There is growing evidence that much of children's aggressive behavior occurs within specific dyadic relationships (Coie and others, 1999; Dodge, Price, Coie, and Christopoulos, 1990). Information processing biases or deficits that are acquired as a possible consequence of community violence exposure (Schwartz and Proctor, 2000; Shahinfar, Kupersmidt, and Matza, 2001) might be intensified by participation in these aggressive exchanges. High-conflict dyadic relationships can provide children with ample opportunities for reinforcement of problematic social-cognitive styles (Egan, Monson, and Perry, 1998).

Through related mechanisms, mutual antipathies might also accelerate trajectories toward other negative social outcomes that are associated with community violence exposure. For example, children who experience neighborhood violence tend to develop behavioral characteristics, such as difficulties regulating negative affect (Schwartz and Proctor, 2000), that are predictive of rebuff and maltreatment by peers. Dyadic animosities could then serve as a social context in which these vulnerable children emerge as persistent targets of bullying (Chapter One, this volume). Peer victimization is generally embedded within a larger social system (Salmivalli, 2001), but bully-victim interactions may occur disproportionately within specific dyads (Dodge, Price, Coie, and Christopoulos, 1990).

Although we did not find a strong pattern of relations between mutual antipathies and the indicators of psychosocial maladjustment, the stressful nature of these dyadic relationships might still be another important factor to consider. For some children, disliking in dyadic relationships could represent a particularly intense and personal form of social rejection (Hartup and Abecassis, 2002). Conflict is also likely to be a central aspect of these enmities with peers (Chapter One, this volume; Dodge, Price, Coie, and Christopoulos, 1990). The distress associated with such difficult social experiences could have an indirect influence on children's adjustment by increasing their susceptibility to the negative effects of other environmental stressors, such as community violence exposure. Resilience will be relatively unlikely when a child is exposed to multiple risk factors (Compas and others, 2001).

A more parsimonious conceptualization might hold that dyadic enmities do not play a direct role in the mechanisms of risk but instead are markers of relevant underlying processes. For example, children who are characterized by impairments in emotion regulation or maladaptive biases in social information processing may be particularly likely to become involved in high-conflict dyadic peer relationships (Dodge, Price, Coie, and Christopoulos, 1990; Hubbard and others, 2001). These deficits could in turn interfere with children's ability to cope with community violence exposure and other urban stressors (Osofsky, 1995). From this perspective, children who frequently become involved in mutual antipathies with peers might be conceptualized as a vulnerable subgroup.

An interesting aspect of our findings is that animosities within dyadic relationships emerged as a more relevant factor than disliking by the peer group as a whole. These results might indicate that the processes associated with heightened vulnerability to community violence exposure are specific to dyadic enmities. An important goal for future investigators will be to examine possible differences in the determinants of peer rejection and mutual antipathies. Such research could help illuminate the underlying mechanisms of risk. In the meantime, the limited availability of relevant descriptive data precludes strong inferences.

Gender differences in the moderating role of mutual antipathies will also require further investigation. We found that the impact of involvement in dyadic animosities on the prediction of some maladjustment indicators (depression, withdrawal, and academic functioning) was different for boys and girls. Our analyses were exploratory in nature and were not driven by a priori theory. However, we might speculate that mutual antipathies could interfere with girls' academic performance by eroding their self-confidence (Sewell, Farley, Manni, and Hunt, 1982) or fostering distracting rumination about interpersonal relationships (Compas, Phares, and Ledoux, 1989). Among boys, mutual antipathies could lead to withdrawal and depression by threatening their social standing in the larger peer group and limiting their opportunities to fulfill their needs for achievement, recognition, and power (see Buhrmester, 1996, for a more detailed discussion of this issue).

Caveats and Future Directions

Several limitations of this research should be kept in mind when evaluating our findings. First, the cross-sectional design of this study does not provide a strong foundation for conclusions regarding causality. This is a concern because some children are likely to be characterized by attributes that predict both violence exposure and maladjustment (Gorman-Smith and Tolan, 1998). For example, children who tend to become involved in high-conflict dyadic relationships may also select into environments in which violence exposure is a high probability. A more complete understanding of the transactional nature of the relevant development phenomena will require longitudinal designs.

Our procedure for assessing mutual antipathies also bears close consideration. Animosities in dyadic peer relationships have only recently become the focus of empirical attention, and a consensus regarding optimal assessment approaches has yet to emerge (see Chapter One, this volume). In this investigation, two children were conceptualized as being involved in a mutual antipathy if they expressed disliking for each other within the context of a limited-choice peer nomination procedure. However, further research may indicate that other approaches, such as unrestricted nominations, yield estimates with greater validity.

A related issue is that our index of mutual antipathies included enmities within both same-sex and mixed-sex dyads. Although there is evidence that the relevant mechanisms of risk can be influenced by the gender composition of the dyad (Abecassis and others, 2002), we lacked sufficient cell size within dyad type to consider this issue fully. We suspect that at this developmental stage, same-gender animosities will be more closely associated with vulnerability to community violence exposure than mixed-gender animosities. The latter type of dyadic relationship may reflect a more normative social process with the majority of antipathies including children of opposite genders (see Hartup and Abecassis, 2002).

Another potential limitation of this study is that our analyses were restricted to a specific class of stressful experiences: community violence exposure by direct victimization. However, in densely populated urban areas, children are likely to be exposed to stress in a number of different domains (for related comments, see Kliewer, Lepore, Oskin, and Johnson, 1998). Similarly, community violence exposure has sometimes been conceptualized as a multidimensional construct, with an emphasis on distinct forms of exposure, such as exposure through violent victimization and through witnessing (Schwartz and Proctor, 2000). In future research on the moderating role of dyadic animosities, it will be important to include more varied assessments that tap a wider array of potential stressors and multiple forms of violence exposure.

In summary, the results of this investigation shed light on the role of children's peer relationships in moderating the outcomes associated with community violence exposure. Children who had numerous mutual antipathies in the school peer group appear to represent a group that is at especially high risk for adjustment difficulties following community violence exposure. Further research, conducted using longitudinal designs, is clearly warranted.

References

Abecassis, M., and others. "Mutual Antipathies and Their Significance in Middle Childhood and Adolescence." *Child Development,* 2002, *73,* 1543–1556.

Aiken, L. S., and West, S. G. *Multiple Regression: Testing and Interpreting Interactions.* Thousand Oaks, Calif.: Sage, 1991.

Bell, C. C., and Jenkins, E. J. "Community Violence and Children on Chicago's South Side." *Psychiatry,* 1993, *56,* 46–54.

Blumstein, A., and Wallman, J. *The Crime Drop in America.* Cambridge: Cambridge University Press, 2000.

Bolger, K. E., Patterson, C. J., and Kupersmidt, J. B. "Peer Relationships and Self-Esteem Among Children Who Have Been Maltreated." *Child Development,* 1998, *69,* 1171–1197.

Buhrmester, D. "Need Fulfillment, Interpersonal Competence, and the Developmental Context of Early Adolescent Friendships." In W. M. Bukowski, A. F. Newcomb, and

W. W. Hartup (eds.), *The Company They Keep*. Cambridge: Cambridge University Press, 1996.

Coie, J. D., and Dodge, K. A. "Aggression and Antisocial Behavior." In W. Damon (ed.), *Handbook of Child Psychology, Vol. 3: Social, Emotional, and Personality* (5th ed.). New York: Wiley, 1997.

Coie, J. D., and others. "It Takes Two to Fight: A Test of Relational Factors and a Method for Assessing Aggressive Dyads." *Developmental Psychology*, 1999, 35, 1179–1188.

Compas, B. E., and others. "Coping with Stress During Childhood and Adolescence: Problems, Progress, and Potential in Theory and Research." *Psychological Bulletin*, 2001, 127, 87–127.

Compas, B. E., Phares, V., and Ledoux, N. "Stress and Coping Preventative Interventions for Children and Adolescents." In L. A. Bond and B. E. Compas (eds.), *Primary Prevention and Promotion in the Schools*. Thousand Oaks, Calif.: Sage, 1989.

Deater-Deckard, K. "Annotation: Recent Research Examining the Role of Peer Relationships in the Development of Psychopathology." *Journal of Child Psychology and Psychiatry and Allied Disciplines*, 2001, 42, 565–579.

Dodge, K. A., Price, J. M., Coie, J. D., and Christopoulos, C. "On the Development of Aggressive Dyadic Relationships in Boys' Peer Groups." *Human Development*, 1990, 33, 260–270.

Egan, S. K., Monson, T. C., and Perry, D. G. "Social-Cognitive Influences on Change in Aggression over Time." *Developmental Psychology*, 1998, 34, 996–1006.

Fitzpatrick, K. M., and Boldizar, J. P. "The Prevalence and Consequences of Exposure to Violence Among African-American Youth." *Journal of the American Academy of Child and Adolescent Psychiatry*, 1993, 32, 424–430.

Gorman-Smith, D., and Tolan, P. "The Role of Exposure to Community Violence and Developmental Problems Among Inner-City Youth." *Development and Psychopathology*, 1998, 10, 101–116.

Hartup, W. W., and Abecassis, M. "Friends and Enemies." In P. K. Smith and C. H. Hart (eds.), *Blackwell's Handbook of Social Development*. Cambridge, Mass.: Blackwell, 2002.

Hill, H. M., and Madhere, S. "Exposure to Community Violence and African American Children: A Multidimensional Model of Risks and Resources." *Journal of Community Psychology*, 1996, 24, 26–43.

Hodges, E.V.E., Boivin, M., Vitaro, F., and Bukowski, W. M. "The Power of Friendship: Protection Against an Escalating Cycle of Peer Victimization." *Developmental Psychology*, 1999, 35, 94–101.

Hodges, E.V.E., Malone, M. J., and Perry, D. G. "Individual Risk and Social Risk as Interacting Determinants of Victimization in the Peer Group." *Developmental Psychology*, 1997, 33, 1032–1039.

Hubbard, J. A., and others. "The Dyadic Nature of Social-Information-Processing in Boys' Reactive and Proactive Aggression." *Journal of Personality and Social Psychology*, 2001, 80, 268–280.

Kliewer, W., Lepore, S. J., Oskin, D., and Johnson, P. D. "The Role of Social and Cognitive Processes in Children's Adjustment to Community Violence." *Journal of Consulting and Clinical Psychology*, 1998, 66, 199–209.

Kovacs, M. "The Children's Depression Inventory." *Psychopharmacology Bulletin*, 1985, 21, 995–998.

Martinez, P., and Richters, J. E. "The NIMH Community Violence Project: II. Children's Distress Symptoms Associated with Violence Exposure." *Psychiatry*, 1993, 56, 22–35.

Osofsky, J. D. "The Effect of Exposure to Violence on Young Children." *American Psychologist*, 1995, 50, 782–788.

Osofsky, J. D., Wewers, S., Hann, D. M., and Fick, A. C. "Chronic Community Violence: What Is Happening to Our Children?" *Psychiatry*, 1993, 56, 36–45.

Overstreet, S., and Braun, S. "A Preliminary Examination of the Relationship Between Exposure to Community Violence and Academic Functioning." *School Psychology Quarterly*, 1999, 14, 380–396.

Parker, J. G., and Asher, S. R. "Peer Relations and Later Personal Adjustment: Are Low Accepted Children at Risk?" *Psychological Bulletin,* 1987, *102,* 357–389.

Richters, J. E., and Martinez, P. E. "Violent Communities, Family Choices, and Children's Chances: An Algorithm for Improving the Odds." *Development and Psychopathology,* 1993, *5,* 609–627.

Salmivalli, C. "Group View on Victimization: Empirical Findings and Their Implications." In J. Juvonen and S. Graham (eds.), *Peer Harassment in School: The Plight of the Vulnerable and Victimized.* New York: Guilford Press, 2001.

Schwartz, D., and Hopmeyer-Gorman. "Community Violence Exposure and Children's Academic Performance." *Journal of Educational Psychology,* 2003, *95,* 163–173.

Schwartz, D., and others. "Friendship as a Moderating Factor in the Pathway Between Early Harsh Home Environment and Later Victimization in the Peer Group." *Developmental Psychology,* 2000, *36,* 646–662.

Schwartz, D., and Proctor, L. J. "Community Violence Exposure and Children's Social Adjustment in the School Peer Group: The Mediating Roles of Emotion Regulation and Social Cognition." *Journal of Consulting and Clinical Psychology,* 2000, *68,* 670–683.

Sewell, T. E., Farley, F. H., Manni, J. L., and Hunt, P. "Motivation, Social Reinforcement and Intelligence as Predictors of Academic Achievement in Black Adolescents." *Adolescence,* 1982, *17,* 647–656.

Shahinfar, A., Kupersmidt, J. B., and Matza, L. S. "The Relation Between Exposure to Violence and Social Information Processing Among Incarcerated Adolescents." *Journal of Abnormal Psychology,* 2001, *110,* 136–141.

Singer, M. I., Anglin, T. M., Song, L. Y., and Lunghofer, L. "Adolescents' Exposure to Violence and Associated Symptoms of Psychological Trauma." *Journal of the American Medical Association,* 1995, *273,* 477–482.

DAVID SCHWARTZ *is an associate professor of psychology at the University of Southern California, Los Angeles.*

ANDREA HOPMEYER-GORMAN *is an associate professor of psychology at Occidental College, Eagle Rock, California.*

ROBIN L. TOBLIN *is a doctoral student in clinical psychology at the University of Southern California, Los Angeles.*

TANIA ABOU-EZZEDDINE *is a doctoral student in clinical psychology at the University of Southern California, Los Angeles.*

4

This chapter addresses the potential implications of mutual antipathies for children's experiences with the peer group as well as the behaviors and perceptions that may drive dyadic disdain.

Describing the Dark Side of Preadolescents' Peer Experiences: Four Questions (and Data) on Preadolescents' Enemies

Jeffrey G. Parker, Bridget K. Gamm

April 2. Carrie told me today to "Go sit on the floor with the dogs where you belong." Have you *ever* heard anything so *mean?* When I told Michelle she said Carrie didn't say that. . . .

April 13. Got in trouble. Carrie kept shooting insults and hid my purse. When I accused her she said no. She is so juvenile. No one believed me. Carrie is just "God" to them. Everyone (Michelle, Tanya, Jen, Heather M., Sarah) sat at Carrie's table and were all friendly and clicky [*sic*]. I think they were talking about me. I'm just going to walk away and not answer her dumb questions for the future. Ms Armstad made me sit away from Michelle for fighting with Carrie.

April 19. If you can believe it Carrie (the *child!*) had the nerve to pull the strap off my purse. When I was doing *nothing*, I repeat, *nothing*, to her. She is not going to get away with it (hopefully!). . . . Michelle and Tanya just said I probably just stepped on it. They said Carrie wouldn't do that. They're just afraid of losing popularity.

We thank the students and staff at the West Branch School, Allport, Pennsylvania, for graciously participating in this study and Alisha Walker, Melanie Roth, and all the fabulous undergraduates who helped with data collection. We are indebted to Amanda Rose for providing us with a copy of the software used to create the sociometric rosters described in this chapter and for assisting us in customizing the software for this project.

> *April 2. . . .* Paid no attention to Carrie today. You could tell she was so
> frustrated not getting anything out of me. . . . Finally Michelle started paying
> attention to me again which made Carrie madder. Revenge!
>
> *April 21.* Finally Carrie got just what she deserved! She asked me why I
> was so ugly and I said "Because I take after you." You could tell she was frus-
> trated. Later when she was bragging I said "Gee, Carrie, it must be great just
> to rank up there with God as far as being perfect." Everybody cracked up.

Carrie and Laura, the seventh-grade girl who wrote the diary entries
above several years ago, are enemies. It appears that each child takes a particular delight in antagonizing the other, a pattern they established almost
a year earlier. Both girls are capable of more successful, positive relations
with others, and their antipathy is directed selectively at one another.
However, as is also apparent, the girls' feuding occasionally envelops the
larger peer group in which they socialize. Moreover, Laura perceives that
her feuding with Carrie has taken a toll on her peer standing. She worries
that she may be losing her close friends to Carrie, and she feels that others
do not understand her antipathy toward Carrie. Indeed, if Laura's inferences
about her peers' reactions are accurate, others do not have the same difficulty with Carrie that she does.

Dyads like Carrie and Laura's are poorly understood. Over the past
twenty-five years, research on children's peer experiences have been carried
out with increasing frequency in many parts of the world. Historically, this
research has reflected two distinct, dominant approaches (Rubin, Bukowski,
and Parker, 1995). The first is oriented toward individual differences in children's group acceptance versus rejection and emphasizes the collective opinion of a group of children about a target child. In this approach, each child's
positive or negative opinion of a target child is given equal weight, making
the construct a summary of the group opinion. Thus, if Carrie's animosity
toward Laura is not widely shared, the chorus of praise the larger peer
group provides will obscure her lone voice of disdain. Moreover, the feelings of the focal child about particular class members do not enter into
the calculation of group acceptance or rejection (Asher, Parkhurst, Hymel,
and Williams, 1996; Bukowski and Hoza, 1989; Parker, Saxon, Asher, and
Kovacs, 1999). Thus, the fact that Laura does not feel similar animosity
toward other individuals who also dislike her is missed.

The second dominant approach emphasizes children's friendship experiences. Unlike group acceptance, friendship is necessarily bilateral and particularized. The views of specific peers are not interchangeable, and one
must assess or assume that both parties to the relationship feel similarly
toward one another (Asher, Parkhurst, Hymel, and Williams, 1996;
Bukowski and Hoza, 1989; Parker, Saxon, Asher, and Kovacs, 1999).
Friendship implies that the individuals involved in the dyad mutually like
one another and have some shared history, and studies of children's friendships emphasize the numbers of friends children have or the varieties of

intimacy, social support, and closeness children experience in these relationships. Thus, the study of children's friendship experiences complements the study of children's group acceptance by adopting the relationship's perspective that the acceptance construct lacks. Yet it is obvious that research on friendship is of limited value in understanding dyads like Carrie and Laura, whose relationship is founded on antipathy rather than affection.

It is difficult to deny that relationships like that of Carrie and Laura are salient to their participants. They are mostly overlooked yet raise interesting questions for developmental researchers and others interested in children's adjustment with peers. In this chapter, we pose four broad research questions related to children's involvement in enemy relationships. Subsequently, we present the methods and findings of research we recently conducted to address these specific aims. It is noteworthy that the topics we address are primarily descriptive questions, reflecting the nascent state of the literature in this area. Our intent is to provide the foundation for more hypothesis-driven research in the future. Toward that end, we close our chapter with some reflections on our findings and some musings on potentially fruitful directions for future research.

Four Questions

Carrie and Laura's relationship may be frustrating and disappointing to those who know them. But it can also prove instructive to others, to themselves, and to developmentalists who puzzle over how such animosities arise, why they persist, and what they tell us about successful and unsuccessful adjustment and development. In this section, we raise four questions for consideration.

What Are the Demographics of Dyadic Disdain? Carrie and Laura's relationship is distinctive, but is it unusual? Very little is known about the prevalence of mutual antipathies among children and adolescents and when these relationships emerge (Hartup and Abecassis, 2002). Among preadolescents and early adolescents in the Netherlands, same-sex mutual antipathies have been identified among 9 to 14 percent of girls and 20 to 25 percent of boys, and mixed-sex antipathies are estimated at 15 to 17 percent for girls and 14 to 16 percent for boys (Abecassis, 1999). Until this volume, the incidence of mutual antipathies among U.S. children and adolescents had yet to be reported in a published manuscript. Accordingly, a first goal of this study was to add to the scarce data on the prevalence of involvement in mutual antipathies among preadolescents.

How Do Enemy Relationships Relate to Preadolescents' Broader Social Adjustment? Laura's suspicion that her broader social welfare may be connected to her difficulties with Carrie is consistent with contemporary recognition that the forces creating and shaping relationships are not purely dyadic or individual (see Rubin, Bukowski, and Parker, 1995). Rather, the embeddedness of relationships in a social network means that individuals must balance their personal and relationship goals against external expectations and exigencies. Moreover, it would hardly be surprising that as children amass more enemies in a group, their overall peer standing will slip. However, such concordances probably partially depend on the number of enemies children typically have. A single or very small number of enemies need not undermine group acceptance if the broader consensus of peer opinion renders them outliers. At the moment, however, few, if any, data exist on this point.

Likewise, relatively little attention has been directed to the issue of how mounting numbers of enemies contribute to stressful peer experiences among children. As Hartup and Abecassis (2002) have recently pointed out, the behavior of enemies toward one another has never been systematically studied, and it is likely that in many instances, enemies simply avoid one another as much as possible. Nonetheless, where accompanied by regular skirmishing, involvement in enemy relationships no doubt carries the risk of increased subjective distress. Indeed, enemy relationships that take this form may account for much of the peer harassment and victimization that children report at school (Juvonen and Graham, 2001).

Accordingly, a second broad goal of the research reported here was to begin an exploration of the links between involvement in enemy relationships and preadolescents' social acceptance, victimization by peers, and feelings of loneliness and social dissatisfaction. While the simple associations among these variables were of interest, we were particularly interested in whether involvement in enemy relationships increased preadolescents' risk in these areas above and beyond the risk that derives from their general peer group rejection.

How Do Preadolescents with Enemies Behave? Little is known about the behavioral qualities of individuals involved in mutual antipathies and how behavior contributes to the formation of these relationships (Hartup and Abecassis, 2002). To be sure, enemy relationships may evolve in such idiosyncratic ways that few aspects of children's general behavioral dispositions predict the extent of their involvement in mutual antipathies. Still, it is difficult to accept that individuals who habitually treat others in disagreeable or offensive ways can avoid generating widespread disdain from others, thereby setting at least the preconditions for extensive involvement in enemy relationships. Indeed, aggression is often cited as grounds for peer rejection (Coie, Dodge, and Kupersmidt, 1990), and relational aggression has also been singled out as having implications for children's experiences with the peer group (Crick, 1997) and in dyadic relationships (Grotpeter and Crick, 1997). By contrast, prosocial behavior is associated with high social status (Coie, Dodge, and Kupersmidt, 1990), suggesting that prosocial children rarely provoke dislike from others or form mutual antipathies.

Jealousy and possessiveness of friends is another behavioral dimension that could be associated with having enemies, although it has been given little consideration in past studies of children's peer relationships. Jealousy is an aversive response to a friend's (or significant other's) association with another person based on the fear that the relationship will end or, at the very least, diminish in quality as a result of the friend's involvement with someone else (Low and Parker, 1999). Highly jealous individuals tend to be less liked and victimized more often by peers than other children (Biggs and Parker, 2001). To the extent that highly jealous individuals see specific other children as threatening to their relationships, they may feel animosity toward them. For their part, individuals who are the target of highly jealous children's animosity may quickly grow weary of this antipathy and come to dislike jealous individuals in return. In this way, jealousy may lie at the root of some mutual antipathies, although this hypothesis has yet to be tested empirically.

Thus, a third goal of the study was to examine the behavioral dispositions of preadolescents involved in mutual antipathies. Specifically, we tested the link between involvement in mutual antipathies and general aggressiveness, relational aggressiveness, prosocial skill, and jealousy and possessiveness surrounding friends.

How Do Preadolescents View Their Enemies? Many contemporary approaches to relationships stress that parties to relationships view one another in particularized ways. Idiosyncratic perceptions sometimes follow from individuals' awareness of their relationship and thus may be regarded as perceptual biases. For example, past research suggests that children's perceptions of another's behavior are influenced by how much they like the target individual (DeLawyer and Foster, 1986; Hymel, 1986; Hymel, Wagner, and Butler, 1990) and the type of relationship they perceive they have with the other (Sumrall, Ray, and Tidwell, 2000). It is unlikely that unique views are entirely in the eyes of the beholder, however. Idiosyncratic perceptions of others presumably also have some bases in reality, reflecting the unique history of the pair together. Indeed, past research has shown that children with uniquely negative views of others also have uniquely negative histories with those individuals (Cillessen and Furguson, 1988; Ledingham and Younger, 1985) and that children tend to respond more negatively to the negative behaviors of disliked peers than to the negative behavior of liked peers (DeLawyer and Foster, 1986).

In the context of mutual antagonistic relationships, it would hardly be surprising if individuals involved in mutually antagonistic relationships hold views of their enemies' behavior that differ from those held by others at large. Mutual enemies may project negative qualities on to one another or may have uniquely negative histories together. Indeed, perceptions and actual behavior may mutually reinforce one another through a feedback loop in which one party's anticipation of negative behavior from the other elicits negative behavior, which in turn strengthens the negative perceptions. Accordingly, a final goal of this study was to explore individuals' perceptions of the behavioral qualities of their enemies and compare those to the perceptions of the general peer group.

An Exploratory Study of Mutual Antipathies in Preadolescence

As noted, a relational approach to dyads like Carrie and Laura can inform us about an apparently salient aspect of children's social experiences that has been overlooked by social scientists until recently. In this section, we present a preliminary study we conducted with a broad aim. Our first goal was to gauge how common these dyadic relationships are for preadolescent boys and girls. Second, we explored the implications of enemy relationships on social adjustment, looking specifically at social acceptance, victimization, and loneliness. Third, we sought to identify some of the behaviors associated with having enemies. Specifically, we explored whether adolescents who form mutual antipathies tend to be any less prosocial and whether they tend to be particularly jealous of their peers or generally and relationally aggressive. Finally, we studied how individuals' perceptions of their enemies' behavior compare the perceptions of the larger peer group as a means to explore the uniqueness of individuals' views of their enemies and of their experiences with those enemies.

Participants and Procedure. The participants were 221 preadolescents living in the rural Northeast United States and enrolled in the seventh through ninth grades of a single middle school. Consistent with the broader demographic makeup of the community, they were overwhelmingly Caucasian and low to middle class in socioeconomic status.

Assessments. Primary assessment took place in the context of a broader research project on social adjustment and friendship during the middle school years and consisted of two group-administered sessions of approximately forty minutes. In these sessions, four broad categories of assessments were obtained: measures of liking, disliking, and group acceptance; assessment of loneliness and social dissatisfaction; peer perceptions of victimization; and peer perceptions of social behavior.

Liking, Disliking, and Group Acceptance. A sociometric rating scale was used to assess participants' affection or animosity toward specific peers as a basis for identifying mutual enemies and mutually liked peers and as a means to gauge participants' general level of acceptance by peers. Specifically, participants were presented with a roster of same-gender classmates and asked to rate the degree of liking they felt toward each peer on a five-point scale. Rosters were constructed using custom software that ensured that the rosters were random across individual participants, with the constraint that every participant's name must appear in the roster of twenty-five of their peers. Participants were permitted to cross out the names of unfamiliar individuals.

Based on these data, mutual antipathies ("enemies") were identified by locating pairs of adolescents who gave one another the strongest possible negative rating ("Do not like at all"). Conversely, mutual affinities were identified by locating pairs of adolescents who gave one another the strongest possible positive rating ("Really like a lot"). Finally, a participant's level of acceptance among peers was determined from the average ratings received from his or her peers, standardized within gender.

Loneliness and Social Dissatisfaction. Participants' feelings of loneliness and social dissatisfaction were assessed using the Loneliness and Social Dissatisfaction Questionnaire (Asher, Parkhurst, Hymel, and Williams, 1990). This questionnaire contains sixteen primary items focused on feelings of loneliness and social dissatisfaction in school and eight distraction items. Participants responded to each item on a five-point scale, indicating the degree to which each statement was a true description of them. Scores were derived from the sum of the sixteen primary items, resulting in scores ranging from 0 to 64, with higher scores indicating greater loneliness and social dissatisfaction (alpha = .90).

Victimization by Peers. Victimization by peers was assessed using four sociometric behavioral nomination items in a larger battery of twenty-one items. Items specific to victimization reflected the tendency for the target to be verbally or physically bullied or harassed by peers (for example, "This person is picked on and teased a lot by other people"). For each item, participants were presented with a roster consisting of a random sample of same-gender classmates and asked to identify any individuals who fit the indicated description. Each individual appeared on the rosters of twenty-five classmates, with an unlimited number of choices of peers permitted for each item. Peer victimization was calculated by first summing the number of nominations received for each victimization item and then dividing by the corresponding number of potential nominators. The resulting percentage scores were then standardized across the sample and averaged across the four items. The internal consistency of the four victimization items was excellent (alpha = .94).

Peer Perceptions of Behavior. Peer reports of participants' behavior in four key domains were assessed as part of the broader twenty-one-item sociometric behavioral nomination battery that included victimization items. Administration and scoring followed the same procedure as the assessment of victimization, including the generation of rosters that permitted each child to be rated by a random sample of twenty-five classmates. The four dimensions of behavior assessed were prosocial skill (four items, alpha = .92), or the tendency to display concern, caring, trust, and helpfulness toward peers; jealousy and possessiveness over friends (four items, alpha = .94), or the tendency to get upset when others do things with one's friends; general aggressiveness (four items, alpha = .90), or the use of verbal or physical harassment including aggressiveness that is nonspecific as to form (for example, "is mean"); and relational aggression (five items, alpha = .94), or the use of overt or covert forms of exclusion and social aggression such as threats to end a friendship and spreading rumors. To avoid confusing a target's inclination to use relational forms of aggression specifically with their broader inclination to be mean in general, participants' general aggressiveness scores were partialed from analyses addressing relational aggression specifically.

Own and Others' Perceptions of One's Enemies and Mutually Liked Peers. Participants' and others' perceptions of enemies and mutually liked peers were assessed.

Own View. For participants involved in mutual antipathies and mutual affinities, nominations of specific enemies for items reflecting prosocial skill, jealousy, and general and relational aggression were tallied in each behavioral domain and then divided by the corresponding number of possible nominations. The resulting percentages were averaged for individuals with more than one enemy. Perceptions of mutually liked others were calculated in an analogous manner.

Peers' Views. Peers' perceptions of the enemies and mutually liked peers of a particular participant were obtained by summing the nominations the enemy or mutually liked other received from peers in each domain of behavior and dividing by the number of nominations possible, excluding actual and potential nominations from the index participant.

Results

First, analyses were conducted to understand the demographics of mutual antipathy. Next, the links between involvement of enemy relationship and loneliness, group acceptance, and peer victimization were examined. Following this, the behavioral adjustment of children with enemy relationships was examined, Finally, participants' perceptions of their enemies and mutually liked peers were compared and contrasted with these individuals' reputations with others who did not consider them enemies.

The Demographics of Dyadic Disdain. It was not uncommon for children to express strong disliking for particular other age-mates. In fact, only about one in eight children (13 percent) did not report strongly disliking (by providing a rating of 1, "Really do not like") at least one individual among the roster of twenty-five random age-mates they were provided. Indeed, on average, children reported strongly disliking about five of the individuals on the roster. There was, however, considerable variability in this regard (SD = 4.3), and at least one individual reported strongly disliking all but one of the individuals listed.

To be considered enemies, it was necessary for such disliking to be reciprocated. Nonetheless, even mutual antipathy appeared commonplace. More than half (58 percent) of all participants were involved in at least one mutual antipathy, and some participants had several enemies (range = 1 to 8). On average, however, children had just over one mutual enemy (M = 1.12). By comparison, more than 80 percent of all children were involved in relationships of high mutual affection, signified by mutual ratings of 5, "Really like a lot." Perhaps encouragingly, children had significantly more mutual affinities (M = 1.58) than mutual antipathies [$t(220)$ = -2.58, $p <$

.01], although this difference is small in absolute terms. It is also worth recalling that children were permitted to rate only a random sample of twenty-five of their same-sex age-mates. Although this number constitutes a substantial proportion of the pool of available same-sex age-mates at the rural school in which the study was conducted, it is likely that the absolute rates of mutual antipathy and affinity are underestimated. Greater involvement in mutual antipathy was modestly but significantly related to fewer mutual affinities [$r(220) = -.22, p < .01$].

Boys and girls were equally likely to be involved in a mutual antipathy [$\chi^2(1) = .01$, ns]. However, significantly more girls (76 percent) than boys (55 percent) had at least one mutual affinity. Repeated measures analysis of variance was used to examine potential gender and age differences in the extent of involvement in mutual antipathies and affinities. Boys and girls had nearly equal numbers of mutual antipathies and affinities on average [$F(1, 215) = 2.35$, ns]. The presence of a significant interaction between grade level and type of relationships, that is, mutual antipathy versus affinity [$F(2, 215)$ 5.67, $p < .004$], suggested changes with age in the balance of the extent of children's involvement with enemies versus mutual affinities. As shown in Figure 4.1, involvement in mutual antipathy declined with age, whereas involvement in mutual affinity increased significantly with age.

Enemies and Peer Group Adjustment. Peer group acceptance and levels of victimization are important gauges of the caliber of preadolescents' adjustment with peers. In addition, preadolescents' reports of loneliness and social dissatisfaction provide an important appraisal of the quality of peer experiences from individuals' subjective point of view. Table 4.1 presents the intercorrelations among these markers of adjustment with peers, as well as the bivariate correlations between these adjustment measures and the extent of children's involvement in dyadic antipathies.

As is apparent from Table 4.1, peer victimization was strongly negatively related to preadolescents' acceptance in the peer group. More important, preadolescents with greater numbers of enemies were both less well liked and more victimized by peers than preadolescents with fewer enemies.

Figure 4.1. Number of Mutual Enemies and Allies, by Grade

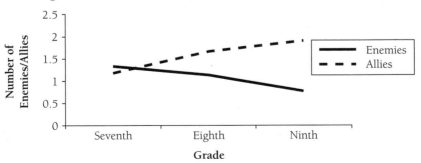

**Table 4.1. Number of Mutual Antipathies and Preadolescents'
Adjustment with Peers and Victimization**

	Victimization by Peers	Loneliness and Social Dissatisfaction	Peer Group Acceptance
Number of mutual antipathies	.19**	.10	−.44**
Victimization by peers		.47**	−.71**
Loneliness and social dissatisfaction			−.43**

Note: ** = Correlation is significant at the .01 level (two-tailed).

The strong association between victimization and peer acceptance raises the question of whether it is the presence of many enemies or simply the low peer standing of these individuals that contributes to their targeting for victimization by peers.

To address this issue, a further analysis that controlled for acceptance using hierarchical multiple regression was conducted. This analysis also offered the potential to explore the possible moderating role of gender. Victimization by peers served as the outcome variable for this analysis. Results revealed a significant main effect of number of reciprocal enemies on victimization after controlling for peer group acceptance (beta = .15, $p <$ .005) but no significant interactions with gender and acceptance. Thus, for both boys and girls, as individuals amassed greater numbers of enemies, they became more frequent targets of peer victimization, over and above the levels of victimization attached to their slipping peer status.

Table 4.1 also shows that poorly accepted and victimized preadolescents reported greater loneliness and social dissatisfaction at school. This result is certainly not surprising. More surprising perhaps is that the number of enemies was not also strongly associated with reports of loneliness and social dissatisfaction (see Table 4.1). This result was confirmed in more thorough analysis that controlled for acceptance using hierarchical regression. This analysis replicated the strong negative association between acceptance and loneliness (beta = −43, $p <$ .001) but yielded no evidence of a significant association between loneliness and number of enemies, either alone or in interaction with acceptance or gender.

Behavioral Adjustment of Preadolescents with Enemies. Consistent with past research, peers understandably disliked preadolescents who lacked social skills or had aggressive behavioral styles. In fact, the simple correlations between acceptance, on the one hand, and prosocial skill and general and relational aggression, on the other, were r = .71, −.36, and −.25, respectively (all $ps <$ .01). Of specific interest here, from the reports of their peers, in comparison to preadolescents with fewer enemies, preadolescents with more enemies were less prosocial [$r(220) = -.27, p < .01$], more relationally [$r(220) = .25, p < .01$] and generally [$r(220) = .28, p < .01$]

aggressive, and more jealous and possessive of friends [$r(220) = .26, p <$ .01]. Again, hierarchical multiple regression was used to investigate these simple associations more thoroughly and, in particular, to disambiguate the influence of behavior on the formation of mutual antipathies from the contributions of behavior to problems of poor acceptance by the larger peer group.

Specifically, four parallel regressions were conducted predicting number of enemies—one for each of the four behavioral predictors. On the first step of these regressions, gender and level of peer acceptance were initially entered as control variables. On subsequent steps, the behavior variable of interest was then entered—first alone and then in interaction with gender and acceptance. Interactions between behavior and gender were explored on the basis of recent assertions that some forms of negative behavior, particularly relational forms of aggression, are more germane to one gender or another. Similarly, interactions between behavior and acceptance were included to explore possible differences in the link between behavior and mutual antipathy as a function of differences in the social capital that individual preadolescents possess as a result of their greater versus lesser integration into the peer group (Coie, 1990). Finally, in the regression of relational aggression on number of enemies, general aggressiveness was entered as a further control variable, as relationally aggressive individuals tend to employ other forms of aggression as well, and our interest in this analysis was in the influence of relational aggression specifically.

Results revealed, by and large, that preadolescents' behavior in the peer group at large was not strongly linked to the extent of their involvement in mutual antipathies. Thus, prosocial preadolescents were not necessarily without enemies once the tendency for these individuals to be better liked in general was taken into consideration (beta = .03, ns). The simple associations that existed between greater involvement in enemy relations and the tendency to engage in general and relational forms of aggression appeared attributable to the tendency for aggressive individuals to also be less well liked by peers rather than anything about their aggressiveness itself. After controlling for gender and acceptance, the betas associated with the prediction of enemies from general and relational aggression were .06 and .13, respectively, and neither was significant. In addition, neither of the two aggression variables nor the measure of prosocial behavior interacted with gender or level of acceptance to predict involvement in enemy relations. The absence of such interactions indicates that not even qualified support was present for a link between these behaviors and involvement in enemy relations.

An exception existed for jealousy. In contrast to the other forms of behavior, participants who were characteristically possessive of their friends and known to grow jealous when others had contact with their friends had more enemies than nonjealous participants, even after controlling for the tendency for jealous participants to be less well liked overall (beta = .18,

$p < .01$). The absence of interactions between jealousy and gender and acceptance further suggests that this relation is relatively robust, holding across genders and regardless of the overall level of acceptance of the individual by peers.

Preadolescents' Perceptions of Their Enemies. A relationships approach would suggest that preadolescents will report more negative experiences with enemies than with nonenemies and that preadolescents' views of others who are enemies will be more negative than the views of preadolescents who do not regard those other individuals as enemies. To explore this issue, preadolescents' views of their enemies' behavior in each of the four behavioral domains were contrasted with their views of mutually liked peers' behavior and also with the perceptions of these same individuals held by their peers. Specifically, a 2 (perspective: target's versus peer group) by 2 (relationship: target's friend versus target's foe) by 2 (gender) analysis of variance was conducted in each of the four behavioral domains, with perspective and relationship serving as repeated factors and gender serving as a between-groups factor. The magnitude of the interaction between perspective and relationship was of primary interest in these analyses, consistent with the expectation of a gap between perceptions of the behaviors of friends versus foes depending on the perspective of the reporter.

Results in each behavioral domain revealed a number of statistically significant lower-order main and interactive effects, including the anticipated interaction between perspective and target. However, in every analysis, a significant three-way interaction between target, perspective, and gender was also present, indicating the need for conditional interpretation by gender. To decompose these interactions, a series of conceptually guided, post hoc simple effects analyses was conducted ($p < .05$). These comparisons suggest the following conclusions.

First, and not surprisingly, preadolescents of both sexes differentiated between the behaviors of enemies versus mutually liked peers in most areas. Thus, preadolescents of both sexes reported that their enemies possessed less prosocial skill and were more generally aggressive than their mutually liked peers, and preadolescent girls (but not boys) regarded their enemies as more jealous and possessive over friends and more relationally aggressive.

However, consistent with specificity of dyadic experiences, these same individuals were not as sharply behaviorally differentiated in the eyes of the larger peer group. Among boys, preadolescents' enemies did have reputations among peers for lower prosocial skills than mutually liked peers. There were not sharp differences between boys' enemies and mutually liked peers in their reputations for jealousy or for relational or general aggression, however. Moreover, girls' enemies and mutually liked peers were not sharply different in any aspect of behavioral reputations with peers.

Finally, comparison of preadolescents' ratings of mutually liked peers to the peer group's ratings of the same individuals suggests that participants' judgments of the behavior of their mutually liked peers generally concurred with the appraisals given to these same individuals by peers at large. Two exceptions exist for girls, who tend to see their mutually liked peers as less jealous and less relationally aggressive than the broader peer group views them. Preadolescents' judgments of their enemies, however, show evidence of being selectively negative. Boys appear to overestimate their enemies' general aggressiveness and underestimate their enemies' prosocial skills, compared to the benchmarks provided by peers. Girls' views of their enemies are even more divergent from the view of these individuals held by the peer group. Specifically, girls tended to view their enemies more negatively and less positively in every domain than did the broader peer group.

Summary and Future Directions

To close, we consider the status of our original four questions and suggest some directions for future inquiry,

The Demographics of Dyadic Disdain. Consistent with past research, mutual antipathy was a common experience for both boys and girls in this study. Although we believe our methodology may have underestimated the number of mutual antipathies and affinities, our estimates were actually higher than those of previous studies investigating mutual antipathies among preadolescents (Abecassis, 1999) and are similar to rates of mutual antipathies for this age group reported in Chapter Two in this volume. Because such estimates may be influenced by methodology and sample, further work is needed on which methods produce the best appraisal of involvement in enemy relationships (see Chapter Six, this volume). Nonetheless, the prevalence of mutual antipathies found in this and in past studies demonstrates that aversive relationships are a common aspect of both boys' and girls' social networks. Thus, these findings support recent calls for further research into the "dark side" of children's peer experiences. In this connection, it is also interesting that other studies (see Chapters Three, Five, and Six, this volume) suggest that rates of mutual antipathies in children of middle childhood age are lower than those we found for children a few years older and entering middle school. At the same time, we observed a decline in mutual antipathies from seventh to ninth grade. Taken together, these trends suggest that rates of mutual antipathy peak in the early preadolescence period. Future studies into children's enemies should include a wider age range or longitudinal design to develop a better picture of how involvement in mutual antipathies and the significance of this involvement may change with age.

Enemies and Peer Group Adjustment. Not surprisingly, adolescents involved in many mutual antipathies were not as well accepted by the peer group as adolescents with few mutual antipathies. Moreover, they also experienced more victimization and bullying by peers, at rates beyond those expected by their marginal group status. These findings support a distinction between involvement in mutual antipathy and general peer group rejection and are consistent with the calls of a growing number of scholars (see Rubin, Bukowski, and Parker, 1995) who have argued that attention to both group- and dyadic-level constructs is necessary for a complete understanding of children's adjustment with peers. Our findings regarding victimization are particularly interesting in that they raise the question of who is victimizing these children. Presumably, a substantial amount of the victimization experienced by adolescents with enemies comes from those enemies themselves, although our data did not address this issue directly. As Hartup and Abecassis (2002) note, very little is understood about enemies' behavior toward one another, and more research on this issue is urgently needed. Even so, our data cast suspicion on at least one proposition about enemies: that they simply avoid or ignore one another. Moreover, in future research, it would be interesting to explore whether victimization by acknowledged enemies has the same emotional and social consequences for children as victimization by the peer group at large.

Relatedly, although number of enemies was associated with being less accepted by the larger peer group and with being victimized, adolescents with enemies were not particularly lonely or lacking in social skills. This finding stands in contrast to the peer rejection literature, which has demonstrated that children who are rejected by the peer group tend to report feeling lonely and dissatisfied with their social experiences (Parker, Saxon, Asher, and Kovacs, 1999). One interpretation of this finding is that the source of victimization has important implications for children's attributions concerning its cause. Victimization by specific individuals who are acknowledged enemies may be more readily discounted than victimization that occurs diffusely and may come from any quarter. If children are victimized strictly by enemies, they may be able to dismiss or discount its significance, make external attributions as to its cause, and encapsulate its emotional consequences. By itself, then, the experience of having enemies need not render children's social life less gratifying, although it understandably might make social life more complex. These issues should be a focus of future research.

Based on her research, Pope (Chapter Six, this volume) concluded that involvement in enemy relationships does not pose challenges for social adjustment beyond the risks posed by peer rejection. Our conclusions are not completely contradictory, however, as our research suggests that some aspects of social adjustment, such as satisfaction with social relationships, do not appear to be related to mutual animosity. Rather, the impact of mutual antipathies appears to be associated with specific aspects of social adjustment, such as victimization by peers. Furthermore, the behaviors that drive mutual antipathies appear to be specific to this kind of relationship and distinct from behaviors associated with peer rejection in general.

Behavioral Adjustment of Preadolescents with Enemies. Although peers disliked preadolescents who lacked social skills or had aggressive behavioral styles, these behavioral difficulties did not necessarily lead to the accumulation of many mutual enemies. Rather, it was the tendency of individuals to be characteristically unusually possessive and jealous over their friends that was most closely related to the development of a large number of mutual animosities. When interpreting these results, it is probably important to keep in mind the reciprocity of animosity inherent in mutual antipathy. Preadolescents with certain negative behavioral dispositions may reliably irritate a wide swath of their peers. However, if they themselves harbor no particular animosity toward specific other peers, it would be misleading to suggest that they are involved in many enemy relationships. Feelings of jealousy are likely to be accompanied by collateral feelings of animosity toward others: specific individuals who are seen as rivals for friends' affection. Jealousy, then, may be a more potent general correlate of enemy involvement than many other behavioral variables because it contributes not only to disagreeable behavior but also to the tendency to target those behaviors toward specific other individuals. However, these conclusions remain tentative due to the correlational nature of this study. Studies with a longitudinal design could shed additional light on this issue.

Preadolescents' Perceptions of Their Enemies. This study took an additional step toward disentangling behavior in these two contexts by examining how adolescents' reports of their enemies' and mutually liked peers' behavior compare to reports from the larger peer group. On the one hand, this study's results can be interpreted as demonstrating a bias in how adolescents view mutually liked versus disliked peers. That is, adolescents may hold unfairly negative views of their enemies and begrudge them positive qualities that they actually possess, while giving their mutually liked peers the benefit of the doubt in some instances. If so, adolescents' views of their enemies, like their views of other types of out-group members (for example, individuals of the opposite gender or another ethnicity), may be said to be subject to perceptions of illusory correlation and other forms of biased stereotyping. If this interpretation is followed, girls in this study would be seen as more discriminating between their enemies' and mutually liked peers' behavior than would boys, as girls' views of their enemies and mutually liked peers differed from the view of the peer group in more behavioral dimensions than did boys' views.

On the other hand, our preferred interpretation is consistent with a growing emphasis on the role of relational or dyadic factors in the occurrence of negative behavior among peers (Coie and others, 1999; Dodge, Price, Coie, and Christopoulos, 1990). Specifically, recent research suggests that relational factors account for at least as much variance in aggressive and negative behavior as the individual characteristics of the targets and perpetrators. The tendency for children in this study to describe their enemies more negatively than did the peer group may in fact reflect their actual history of interaction with these individuals who have behaved selectively toward them. Following this interpretation, this study provides evidence that both boys and girls with enemies are selectively cruel toward their enemies and that girls are additionally jealous and relationally aggressive in these relationships. If these behaviors are specifically directed toward enemies, they may go undetected by the peer group, thus accounting for differences between individual and peer group views.

Regardless of whether adolescents' perceptions of their enemies' behavior reflect bias or an actual history, how they view their enemies has implications for understanding how mutual antipathies are maintained. Because adolescents have negative views of their enemies, they are likely to anticipate continued negative behavior from their enemies (Hymel, 1986). In addition, due to these negative views, they are likely to react more negatively to their enemies' behavior regardless of whether that behavior is positive or negative (see DeLawyer and Foster, 1986). Thus, mutual antipathies could perpetuate themselves through a feedback loop in which enemies' anticipation of negative behavior from each other elicits negative behavior, which strengthens the negative perceptions enemies have of each other. This study provides initial support for the existence of these dynamics by demonstrating that adolescents have a particularly negative view of their enemies compared to the view of the larger peer group. Whether mutual antipathies are maintained by such a negative feedback loop has yet to be determined through further study.

Mutual antipathies such as in the relationship between Laura and Carrie have been a much-ignored aspect of children's social worlds until recently. Yet the prevalence of these relationships suggests that they are a fairly normative experience for children and an important piece in their social network. Furthermore, children's experiences in these relationships appear to have important implications for social adjustment and development that are distinct from rejection by the larger peer group. Future studies should examine the mechanisms by which experiences with enemies shape children's experiences with other peers and affect how they perceive their social worlds. How enemies view and behave toward each other also warrant further study because their perceptions and behaviors have possible implications for how these relationships are formed and maintained.

References

Abecassis, M. "I Dislike You and You Dislike Me: Prevalence and Developmental Significance of Mutual Antipathies Among Preadolescents and Adolescents." Unpublished doctoral dissertation, University of Minnesota, 1999.

Asher, S. R., Parkhurst, J. T., Hymel, S., and Williams, G. A. "Peer Rejection and Loneliness in Childhood." In S. R. Asher and J. D. Coie (eds.), Peer Rejection in Childhood. Cambridge: Cambridge University Press, 1990.

Biggs, B. K., and Parker, J. G. "Adolescents' Jealousy and Possessiveness of Friends: Social, Behavioral, and Personal Correlates." Poster presented at the biennial meeting of the Society for Research in Child Development, Minneapolis, Minn., 2001.

Bukowski, W. M., and Hoza, B. "Popularity and Friendship: Issues in Theory, Measurement, and Outcome." In T. J. Berndt and G. W. Ladd (eds.), *Peer Relations in Child Development.* New York: Wiley, 1989.

Cillessen, T., and Furguson, T. J. "Self-Perpetuation Processes in Children's Peer Relationships." In B. H. Schneider, G. Attili, J. Nadel, and R. P. Weissberg (eds.), *Social Competence in Developmental Perspective.* Norwell, Mass.: Kluwer, 1998.

Coie, J. D. "Toward a Theory of Peer Rejection." In S. R. Asher and J. D. Coie (eds.), *Peer Rejection in Childhood.* Cambridge: Cambridge University Press, 1990.

Coie, J. D., and others. "It Takes Two to Fight: A Test of Relational Factors and a Method for Assessing Aggressive Dyads." *Developmental Psychology,* 1999, *35,* 1179–1188.

Coie, J. D., Dodge, K. A., and Kupersmidt, J. B. "Peer Group Behavior and Social Status." In S. R. Asher and J. D. Coie (eds.), *Peer Rejection in Childhood.* Cambridge: Cambridge University Press, 1990.

Crick, N. R. "The Role of Overt Aggression, Relational Aggression, and Prosocial Behavior in the Prediction of Children's Future Social Adjustment." *Child Development,* 1997, *67,* 2317–2327.

DeLawyer, D. D., and Foster, S. L. "The Effects of Peer Relationships on the Functions of Interpersonal Behavior of Children." *Journal of Clinical Child Psychology,* 1986, *15,* 127–133.

Dodge, K. A., Price, J. M., Coie, J. D., and Christopoulos, C. "On the Development of Aggressive Dyadic Relationships in Boys' Peer Groups." *Human Development,* 1990, *33,* 260–270.

Grotpeter, J. K., and Crick, N. R. "Relational Aggression, Overt Aggression, and Friendship." *Child Development,* 1997, *67,* 2328–2338.

Hartup, W. W., and Abecassis, M. "Friends and Enemies." In P. K. Smith and C. H. Hart (eds.), *Blackwell Handbook of Childhood Social Development.* Cambridge, Mass.: Blackwell, 2002.

Hymel, S. "Interpretation of Peer Behavior: Affective Bias in Childhood and Adolescence." *Child Development,* 1986, *57,* 431–445.

Hymel, S., Wagner, E. and Butler, L. J. "Reputational Bias: View from the Peer Group." In S. R. Asher and J. D. Coie (eds.), *Peer Rejection in Childhood.* Cambridge: Cambridge University Press, 1990.

Juvonen, J., and Graham, S. (eds.). *Peer Harassment in School: The Plight of the Vulnerable and Victimized.* New York: Guilford Press, 2001.

Ledingham, J. E., and Younger, A. J. "The Influence of the Evaluator on Assessments of Children's Social Skills." In B. H. Schneider, K. H. Rubin, and J. E. Ledingham (eds.), *Children's Peer Relations: Issues in Assessment and Intervention.* New York: Springer-Verlag, 1985.

Low, C., and Parker, J. G. "Defining and Assessing Children's Jealousy over Friends: Development and Evaluation of the Friendship Jealousy Questionnaire." Poster presented at the biennial meetings of the Society for Research in Child Development, Albuquerque, N.M., 1999.

Parker, J. G., Saxon, J., Asher, S. R., and Kovacs, D. "Dimensions of Children's Friendship Adjustment: Implications for Studying Loneliness." In K. J. Rotenberg and S. Hymel (eds.), *Loneliness in Childhood and Adolescence.* Cambridge: Cambridge University Press, 1999.

Rubin, K. H., Bukowski, W. A., and Parker, J. G. "Peer Interactions, Relationships, and Groups: A Developmental Perspective." In W. Damon (series ed.) and N. Eisenberg (ed.), *Handbook of Child Psychology Vol. 3: Social, Emotional, and Personality Development.* (5th ed.) New York: Wiley, 1995.

Sumrall, S. G., Ray, G. E., and Tidwell, P. S. "Evaluations of Relational Aggression as a Function of Relationship Type and Conflict Setting." *Aggressive Behavior*, 2000, 26, 179–191.

JEFFREY G. PARKER *is an associate professor and public scholarship associate in the Department of Psychology at Pennsylvania State University, University Park.*

BRIDGET K. GAMM *is a doctoral student in the clinical child psychology program at the University of Kansas, Lawrence.*

5

This analysis of third and fourth graders suggests that enemy relationships are common, often of short duration, and partially reflective of negative behavior patterns between boys and girls in elementary school.

Enemies in the Gendered Societies of Middle Childhood: Prevalence, Stability, Associations with Social Status, and Aggression

Philip C. Rodkin, Ruth Pearl, Thomas W. Farmer, Richard Van Acker

> . . . . I do not look upon affection, or anger, or any other particular mode of feeling, as in itself good or bad, social or antisocial, progressive or retrogressive. It seems to me that the essentially good, social, or progressive thing, in this regard, is the organization and discipline of all emotions by the aid of reason, in harmony with a developing general life, which is summed up for us in conscience. That this development of the general life is such as to tend ultimately to do away with hostile feeling altogether, is not clear. . . . That it ought to disappear is certainly not apparent.
> —C. H. Cooley (1922)

Early research on social behavior viewed hostility and animosity as normal, even inevitable, outgrowths of the individual's vigorous participation in society. For Cooley (1922), dislike and enmity—along with love, friendship, and kindness—were for both children and adults complementary parts

The research reported in this chapter was supported by the U.S. Department of Education, Office of Special Education Research Programs H023C70103 to Ruth Pearl (PI), Thomas W. Farmer, Philip C. Rodkin, and Richard Van Acker. The views in this chapter are ours and do not necessarily represent those of the granting agency. We thank the schools and children who worked with us in this research.

of a generally developing sense of self that could take on a more or less healthy whole. (See also H. S. Sullivan, 1953, for intrapsychic views of the good-me, bad-me, and not-me.) The notion of mutual antipathies as a danger signal for later maladjustment was absent in Cooley's writings without a larger context of knowing toward whom negativity was directed and why. In contrast, Cooley did recognize the great danger of mutual dislike at the group level, writing that the "brutal self-assertion of one who knows his fellows only as objects of suspicion and hostility" (p. 210) damaged what could potentially be a healthy and humane national identity, giving in-group pride a bad name. Moreno's original presentation of the sociometric method (1934) bears similarity to Cooley's ideas about dislike. Moreno (1934) conceptualized liking and disliking (or attraction and repulsion) as two fundamental components of judgment, not antithetical but complementary sentiments whose common antitheses were indifference and apathy (Cillessen and Bukowski, 2000). Moreno (1943) focused on the impact of the overall configurations of positive and negative sentiments on the mental health of the collective social unit—hence, his belief in national psychotherapy and his unique call for sociometrically testing whole communities and reshuffling their populations. This theme that negative sentiments are normal at the level of the individual but problematic at the level of the group arises also in the balance and exchange theories of post–World War II social psychology. Heider (1958) wrote of negative and positive valuations of people and objects as natural, everyday aspects of naive psychology; he was more concerned with whether the relationship among a person's likes and dislikes was internally harmonious than with whether the likes or dislikes predominated. As with Cooley and Moreno, dislike had little meaning apart from the identity of who was disliked and the larger situation in which one's dislikes were embedded.

Thus, social theory and research over the first half of the twentieth century included negative sentiments as a matter of course. Dislike and antipathy were natural complements of positive feelings, and the dangers of dislike revolved around social harmony more than individual mental health. Enmity may simply have been too common to be seen as a significant risk, at least without the added punch of race, class, and group (Clark and Clark, 1947). From the 1950s to the 1970s, interest in dislike and antipathy was an early casualty of the more general decline in peer research (but see Sherif, 1956). Cillessen and Bukowski (2000) note that negative relationships were among the first aspects of Moreno's sociometric theory (1934) to fade away. Part of the reason had to do with ethical difficulties in asking children whom they liked least. Gronlund (1959, p. 47) recommended that "rejection choices" be eliminated wherever possible, changing the wording of negative questions to whom students would "choose last" for an activity rather than whom they least preferred or did not want as associates. Advances in sociometric methodology, including alternative procedures for identifying rejected status children (Asher and Dodge, 1986), further reduced interest in negative nominations. Nonetheless, Coie, Dodge, and Coppotelli's remark that "there is much that cannot be learned about social relations among children without introducing the negative choice issue" (1982, p. 567) echoes loudly in the study of children's antipathies, which represents an innovative, virtually unexplored direction for peer relations research despite a long intellectual background.

We present our contribution to the study of childhood antipathies in two sections. First, we provide descriptive information about enemy relationships, drawing from a longitudinal study in which children were assessed in the spring of third grade and the fall and spring of fourth grade. Second, we examine individual differences in social status and aggressive behavior between children with none, one, or more than one antipathy. We also consider whether children who gain or lose enemies over the school year show consequent shifts in their social status or aggressive behavior. The goal is to understand better whether children with enemies are marginalized in the classroom social structure (that is, are unpopular or aggressive), or whether involvement in antipathies characterizes a wide variety of children dispersed throughout the classroom status hierarchy. The classical social relations literature suggests that negative interpersonal relationships, as a normal feature of social life, should include popular and unpopular, aggressive and nonaggressive children alike.

We examined these issues in analyses of a combined cross-sectional and longitudinal sample. Children were assessed in the spring of their third-grade year and again in the fall and spring of the fourth grade. For all assessment waves, children were sampled from twenty-nine classrooms in seven schools and two school districts. Schools were located in a suburban section of a major midwestern metropolitan area. In third grade, seven of the twenty-nine classrooms were combined third-fourth grades and two were combined second-third grades. In the fourth grade, six were combined third-fourth, and six were combined fourth-fifth grade classrooms. In cases of mixed-grade classes, older and younger classmates were included with the target children in our analyses; in this study, we did not examine moderating effects of mixed-grade classrooms. We followed 315 children (149 boys, 166 girls) for all three assessments and 165 children (82 boys, 83 girls) from the fall to spring of the target children's fourth grade; 122 children (57 boys, 65 girls) participated only during the spring of the target children's third-grade assessment. Some of the children who did not continue their participation in this study to the second and third assessment waves were second or fourth graders in classrooms mixed with third graders. In spring third grade, the participation rate for the target children was 72.0 percent. The ethnic distribution was European American, 65.9 percent; Latina/o, 18.7 percent; African American, 6.1 percent; Asian, 5.4 percent; and 3.9 percent had other ethnic nationalities. Participation rates and ethnic composition for the target children in the fall and spring fourth-grade assessments closely approximated the spring third-grade assessment.

Mutual antipathies (or enemies, as we use these terms interchangeably) were determined through reciprocated liked-least nominations, where children were simply asked to nominate up to three children whom they "liked least." Children were also asked to nominate up to three children whom they "liked most." Importantly, the nomination pool for this study consisted of only other study participants. Children were requested to nominate only other study participants whose names were on a class roster included with the study protocol. Student surveys, of which the liked-least and liked-most questions were a part, were administered in a group format during regular classroom time and took approximately forty-five minutes.

Retention rates were calculated between spring third-grade and both fourth-grade assessments and between the two fourth-grade assessments. We gave particular attention to possible retention rate differences between children with and without enemies. For boys, retention was 72.8 percent between third-grade spring and fourth-grade fall (75.5 percent for third-grade children with at least one enemy), 70.9 percent between third-grade spring and fourth-grade spring (73.4 percent for third-grade children with at least one enemy), and 96.9 percent between fourth-grade fall and fourth-grade spring (97.7 percent for fourth-grade fall children with at least one enemy). Retention rates for girls, with the retention rate for girls with at least one enemy included in parentheses, were 71.9 percent (68.9 percent) between third-grade spring and fourth-grade fall, 70.0 percent (66.7 percent) between third-grade spring and fourth-grade spring, and 96.0 percent (95.7 percent) between fourth-grade fall and fourth-grade spring. These percentages suggest that children with enemies were no more likely to drop out of the study than were children without enemies.

Descriptive Characteristics of Middle Childhood Enemy Relationships

We calculate the prevalence of antipathies in our sample, relative proportions of same- and cross-sex enemy dyads, and the stability of enemy relationships between and across school years. We consider the results of our analyses in the light of comparable estimates from other contributors to this volume.

Prevalence of Enemy Relationships. Estimates of the prevalence of enemy relationships help frame discussion of whether having an enemy is a relatively normal versus abnormal aspect of interpersonal relations for middle childhood boys and girls. Examination of developmental trends provides researchers and school personnel with information on whether mutual antipathies rise, fall, or maintain themselves from the third- to fourth-grade years. We begin by calculating the proportion of boys and girls who participated in zero, one, or more than one enemy relationship during the spring of third grade and the fall and spring of fourth grade.

Table 5.1 presents our results. The data in Table 5.1 indicate that between approximately 20 and 40 percent of third and fourth graders were involved in at least one antipathy, with a much smaller percentage (between 4 percent and 14 percent) having two or three enemies. Enemy relationships appeared to become more common in the fourth grade. We tested this possibility among children for whom we had complete longitudinal data by performing two repeated measures ANOVAs, for boys and girls, using the number of a child's enemies at third-grade spring, fourth-grade fall, and fourth-grade spring as dependent variables. Two planned contrasts were examined: (1) a between-grade contrast comparing third- to fourth-grade values (weights: $1 - 0.5 -0.5$) and (2) a within-grade contrast comparing fourth-grade fall and spring values (weights: $0\ 1\ -1$). Omnibus F's showed a significant effect for boys [$F(2,147) = 3.97$, $p = .02$] and a trend for girls [$F(2,164) = 2.76$, $p = .07$] with significant between-grade [boys: $F(1,148) = 7.97$, $p = .0005$; girls: $F(1,165) = 5.09$, $p = .03$] but nonsignificant within-grade contrasts. Following up on the between-grade effect, two-sample t tests compared the enemies of children assessed only during the third grade with those of children who began their participation in the fall of fourth grade. Significant effects were revealed for boys ($t(137) = 1.95$, $p = .05$) but not girls. There were no significant effects when changes in the number of enemies over the fourth-grade year were examined for children who began their participation in the fourth grade.

The prevalence estimates reported here are broadly comparable with those of other investigations of middle childhood enemy relationships. Abecassis and others (2002), in a large-scale longitudinal study of Dutch fourth to sixth graders, reported that between 15 and 25 percent of boys and 8 and 17 percent of girls participated in an enemy relationship, with boys involved in more same-sex but not cross-sex antipathies than girls. Other studies with American children have somewhat higher prevalence estimates than Abecassis and others and suggest increased involvement in antipathies with age. Pope (Chapter Six, this volume) found that 28 percent of third

Table 5.1. Proportion of Girls and Boys with Mutual Antipathies from Spring Third Grade to Spring Fourth Grade (Combined Longitudinal and Cross-Sectional Data)

	Third-Grade Spring		Fourth-Grade Fall		Fourth-Grade Spring	
Number of Enemies	Girls	Boys	Girls	Boys	Girls	Boys
None	.78 (180)	.76 (157)	.73 (182)	.62 (144)	.69 (173)	.60 (138)
One	.18 (41)	.16 (32)	.20 (49)	.24 (55)	.20 (49)	.26 (61)
Two or three	.04 (10)	.08 (17)	.07 (18)	.14 (32)	.11 (27)	.14 (32)
Total	1.0 (231)	1.0 (206)	1.0 (249)	1.0 (231)	1.0 (249)	1.0 (231)

Note: The number in parentheses indicates number of children.

and fourth graders and 38 percent of fifth and sixth graders had at least one enemy. Schwartz, Hopmeyer-Gorman, Toblin, and Abou-ezzeddine (Chapter Three, this volume) provide a prevalence estimate of 29 percent for third to fifth graders, and Card and Hodges (Chapter Two, this volume) reported that 48 percent of their sample of fourth through eighth graders had a mutual antipathy. Turning to the adolescent years, Parker and Gamm (Chapter Four, this volume) found that over half of their seventh- to ninth-grade sample had an enemy. Considered together with our sample, these data suggest that negative relationships increasingly become a normal, if unpleasant, element of social life as children, particularly boys, traverse the middle to late elementary school years.

Gender Segregation and Mutual Antipathies. Gender segregation may be the signature phenomenon of middle childhood social development. Boys and girls hardly ever form reciprocated friendships, and the few opposite-sex friendships that do exist may not be as strongly related to social competence as same-sex friendships (Vaughn and others, 2001). Boys and girls rarely participate in mixed-sex groups unless group composition is dictated by the teacher or another authority figure (Maccoby, 1998; Martin and Fabes, 2001; Thorne, 1993). Social network analyses show that the internal structures of boys' and girls' groups differ from one another, with boys' groups being larger, more cohesive, and more stratified on the basis of power and status (Benenson and others, 2001). Boy and girl peer groups can also diverge on the behavioral and social characteristics that children support and emulate. Groups of boys tend to value toughness and competition, while material possessions, cooperation and intimacy, and appearance may have the strongest links to popularity for girls. Maccoby (1998) further suggests that there is an entrenched power asymmetry in favor of boys. Although there are many similarities between boys and girls, gender segregation in middle childhood is impossible to ignore, and thus is a natural candidate for descriptive analysis in the emerging study of children's enemy relationships.

Abecassis and others (2002) reported that cross-sex antipathies were almost as common as same-sex antipathies, but otherwise not much evidence is available on the relative frequency of cross- and same-sex enemy dyads. Schneider (2001) reports that same-sex enemies predominate among adults but gave no comparable data for children. Ethnographies on the gendered cultures of middle childhood suggest two main possibilities. One is that there are relatively few opposite-sex antipathies because there is very little interaction between the gendered separate worlds of middle childhood (Eder, Evans, and Parker, 1995; Thorne, 1993). In this view, there is a buffer zone of neutrality and ignorance between the sexes. Another possibility is that mutual antipathies between girls and boys are relatively frequent because the "borderwork" between boy and girl cultures can be a highly charged, uncomfortable, unbalanced, ill-defined affiliative zone (Adler and Adler, 1998; Maccoby, 1998). Sometimes antipathy between a boy and a girl may be the only socially legitimate way to express deep feelings toward a member of the opposite sex. Adler and Adler (1998, p. 166) wrote that "manifest dislike" between girls and boys was "tempered with a sexual tension or interest that lingered just below the surface." Maccoby (1998) makes similar remarks. Other times, opposite-sex enmities may be reflective of a polluted social dynamic between the sexes. For example, Underwood, Schockner, and Hurley (2001) placed eight-, ten-, and twelve-year-old children in an experimental scenario where they were teased by either a same- or opposite-sex confederate while losing at a computer game. Observational data taken during the teasing episode indicated that children who were teased by opposite- as compared to same-sex peers showed more negative facial expressions, made more negative remarks, and displayed more negative gestures. Postexperimental interviews revealed that children liked and wanted to be friends with the provocateur less when they were of the opposite sex. Many researchers agree that between-sex encounters, particularly in the third- through fifth-grade years, are unduly negative and strictly regulated by social norms.

We tabulated the frequency of mutual antipathies among girls, among boys, and between boys and girls. The results are presented in Table 5.2. The likelihood that children participated in same- versus opposite-sex mutual antipathies was uncorrelated at all assessment periods save one [third- grade boys: $r(206) = 0.20$, $p < .001$]. At each assessment period, we conducted simple chi-square analyses to determine whether the relative frequency of male, female, and opposite-sex dyads varied from chance (respectively, 25 percent, 25 percent, and 50 percent, with minor adjustment for the higher number of girls than boys in our sample). Results indicated that enemy dyads were proportionately distributed over gender composition during the spring of third grade [$\chi^2(2, N = 66) < 1$] but not in either of the fourth-grade assessments [$\chi^2(2)s < 12$, p's $< .01$]. The distribution of enemy dyads in fourth grade had a higher proportion of male dyads and a lower proportion of opposite-sex dyads than would be expected by chance or when compared to the spring third-grade assessment [$\chi^2(2)s < 6.67$, p's $< .05$]. Still, when it comes to gender and middle childhood, the chance null

Table 5.2. Distribution of Enemy Relationships Among Boys, Among Girls, and Between Boys and Girls: Spring Third Grade, Fall Fourth Grade, and Spring Fourth Grade

	Assessment Period		
Gender Composition	Third-Grade Spring	Fourth-Grade Fall	Fourth-Grade Spring
Two boys	.27 (18)	.37 (44)	.35 (46)
Two girls	.21 (14)	.21 (25)	.24 (31)
Boy-girl	.52 (34)	.42 (50)	.41 (54)
Total	1.0 (66)	1.0 (119)	1.0 (131)

Note: The number in parentheses indicates the number of children.

hypothesis is statistically convenient but substantively unrealistic. Even in the fourth grade, over 40 percent of mutual animosities were between a boy and a girl. In comparison, the proportion of mixed-sex friendships and peer groups in middle childhood is far lower (for instance, see Cairns, Leung, Buchanan, and Cairns, 1995; Haselager, Hartup, van Lieshout, and Riksen-Walraven, 1998). Mutual antipathy, then, has great promise as one of the only types of childhood relationships that can tap into the quality (or lack thereof) of boy and girl cultural borderwork.

Stability of Mutual Antipathies. Two aspects of stability were considered. First, we examined the likelihood that children would keep a relationship of antipathy with the same individual over fourth grade. Second, we explored the possibility that children would show stability in being engaged in single mutual antipathy, albeit with different individuals over time.

Findings on the stability of specific dyads were mixed. Given attrition, 114 of the 119 enemy dyads identified in the fall of fourth grade (see Table 5.2) had the potential to remain intact to the spring assessment. Only 19 (17 percent) were actually identified during both assessments. Stability estimates did rise when analysis was restricted to children who maintained at least one mutual antipathy, even if with a different peer in fall and spring. Between 44 and 50 percent of children who maintained a same-sex enemy, and between 55 and 63 percent of children who maintained an opposite-sex enemy had the same child as an enemy throughout the fourth grade.

Indeed, stability in mutual antipathies becomes easier to observe when viewed as involving the maintenance of some reciprocated dislike, even if not to the same peer. We constructed contingency tables comparing children who did versus did not have at least one antipathy in the fall and spring of fourth grade. There were strong, significant associations for boys [$\chi^2(1, N = 231) = 7.21$, $r = 0.18$, $p = .007$] and girls [$\chi^2(1, N = 249) = 11.43$, $r = 0.22$, $p < .001$]. In Table 5.3, we consider stability in opposite- and same-sex antipathies separately and present likelihood ratio estimates and correlation coefficients from a series of two by two chi-square analyses. The results of Table 5.3 suggest stability for girls and boys in their likelihood of maintaining enemies of a particular sex. The strongest within-year continuity was for girls' same-sex enemies, possibly stemming from the long-term nature of relationally aggressive themes that may characterize girls' likes and dislikes.

We conducted between-grade stability analyses for target children. Following the procedure outlined, we constructed contingency tables comparing girls and boys who did and did not have enemies in spring third- and fall fourth-grade assessments. There were no significant between-grade associations for girls or boys in same-sex antipathies [$\chi^2(1)$'s < 1.5, p's > .2] or in having an enemy regardless of gender [$\chi^2(1)$'s < 1]. However, boys who participated in an opposite-sex antipathy in third grade were prone to have an opposite-sex antipathy in the fall of fourth grade [$\chi^2(1, N = 149) = 4.54$,

Table 5.3. Within-Grade Continuity in the Likelihood of Maintaining an Enemy Relationship with Same- and Opposite-Sex Peers

	Fall Fourth-Grade Enemy Dyad							
	Girls				Boys			
Spring Fourth-Grade Enemy Dyad	Same Sex		Opposite Sex		Same Sex		Opposite Sex	
	χ^2	r	χ^2	r	χ^2	r	χ^2	r
Same sex	25.7**	0.36	0.46	0.04	5.45*	0.16	0.21	0.03
Opposite sex	0.02	0.01	4.95*	0.15	0.60	0.05	4.87*	0.16

Note: Values in the chi-square column are likelihood ratio estimates with a chi-square distribution. $*p < .05. **p < .001.$

$r = 0.18$, $p = .03$]. Surprisingly, girls who participated in an opposite-sex antipathy in third grade were unlikely to have an opposite-sex antipathy in the fall of fourth grade [$\chi^2(1, N = 166) = 5.51$, $r = \chi 0.14$, $p = .02$]. The number of post hoc tests conducted in connection with the counterintuitive findings qualifies our interpretation of these results. One possibility for future research is that some boys may be inclined to develop antipathies toward girls, with girls learning to avoid these relationships as they experience them.

To complicate matters further, the stability of enemy relationships weakens considerably but does not vanish when general dislike (that is, proportion of classroom liked least nominations) is considered. Transferring to an analytic procedure that uses an ordinal-interval (that is, 0, 1, 2, 3) measure of enemies, we examined between-grade stability through a series of multiple linear regressions (MLRs) with fourth-grade fall enemies as the dependent variable and third-grade spring enemies, third-grade spring dislike, and their interaction as dependent variables. Opposite- and same-sex enemies were considered along with their aggregate. For both boys and girls, fourth-grade fall same-sex enemy relationships were associated with third-grade spring liked-least nominations [boys: $F(1, 113) = 7.39$, $p < .01$; girls: $F(1,129) = 4.61$, $p < .05$]. No other significant effects appeared. Then we examined within-grade stability, replacing third-grade spring and fourth-grade fall with their corresponding fourth-grade fall and spring measures. For boys, fourth-grade fall liked-least nominations were associated with fourth-grade spring opposite-sex, same-sex, and aggregated enemies [$F(1,227)$'s > 9, p's < .01]. There were no other significant effects for boys. Liked-least nominations in fall were also associated with girls' opposite-sex, same-sex, and aggregated enemies in spring [$F(1,245)$'s > 5, p's < .05]. In addition, girls' fourth-grade fall same-sex enemies were associated uniquely with their spring same-sex enemies [$F(1,227) = 14.8$, $p < .001$]. Finally, in the analysis of girls' opposite-sex enemies, the interaction between fall liked-least nominations and fall opposite-sex enemies reached significance

$[F(1,227) = 5.06, p = .02]$, where there was same-sex enemy stability only for highly disliked girls.

What messages can we take from this array of significant and non-significant findings on the stability of children's mutual antipathies? One clear message is that specific relationships of dislike can change quickly. The same is also true of friendships. Cairns and Cairns (1994, p. 95) report fourth-grade data from their Carolina Longitudinal Study, suggesting that friendships have "a very short half-life" and are "remarkably fluid," with the probability of maintaining a best friendship from one year to the next being only around 20 percent. Cairns and Cairns (1994) argue that that the functions of "fickle" friendships include self-definition and identity formation during middle childhood and early adolescence. As Abecassis (Chapter One, this volume) points out, surely some of these same adaptive developmental functions can apply to children's antipathies. Indeed, antipathies may be even more dynamic and less stable than friendships. Disliking is a more complicated sentiment than liking. Liking leads to the mutually supportive actions of benefiting and supporting, but disliking often leads to a challenging and imbalance-inducing decision between harming and withdrawing, fight and flight (Heider, 1958). Flight and other strategies that lower the frequency of negative interactions make mutual dislike inherently less stable than reciprocated liking. According to Homans (1961), exceptions to the fleeting nature of enmities occur when authority figures do not allow individuals to cut off interaction, or when status and power differences between interactants enable asymmetrical relationships of mutual antipathy to be maintained.

Viewed in this light, any evidence of stability in antipathies is disturbing because it suggests that at least one member of the enemy dyad cannot or does not want to leave. For example, the greater stability of mutual antipathies for children who are generally disliked may be connected to their limited range of affiliative space in the classroom. Some boys may prefer to maintain at least one opposite-sex enemy. Some girls may become locked into a relationally aggressive power dynamic that takes time to play out. Each of these possibilities is speculative and should be followed up in future research. From the standpoint of risk, the chronicity of these kinds of cases should be differentiated from the larger pool of enemy relationships that are more transient and perhaps better suited for issues of collective health (for instance, borderwork between boy and girl cultures) than individual maladjustment (see also Ladd and Ladd, 2001).

Enemies and Peer Rejection

The little research that exists on children with enemies suggests that they resemble many rejected children, with widespread unpopularity and high levels of aggression. Hayes, Gershman, and Bolin (1980) asked preschoolers from middle-class homes why they disliked some peers. Almost all of the preschoolers singled out aggression, rule violations, and aberrant behavior. Frude's analysis (1993) of hatred between children focuses heavily on the peer-rejected child. Mutual antipathies and peer rejection are mathematically related since both require that the child receive at least one liked-least nomination. The question naturally arises as to whether there is any distinction between the constructs of enmity and rejection. According to recent research, there is. Abecassis and others (2002) report in their large Dutch sample that same-sex antipathies are associated with antisocial behavior and withdrawal beyond the effects of rejection. Similarly, mixed-sex antipathies were related to aggression in boys and victimization, submissiveness, and depression in girls after controlling statistically for effects of peer dislike.

In this section, we compare children who have no enemies to those who have one or more than one on peer and teacher reports of, popularity, and aggression. We also compare children who pick up versus lose enemies over the fourth-grade school year. In all of these analyses, we considered the moderating role of peer rejection. We also took account of whether children's enemies were same or opposite sex. Teacher ratings of popularity and aggression were taken from the Interpersonal Competence Scale–Teacher (ICS-T) (for a detailed explanation of the psychometric properties of this scale, see Cairns, Leung, Gest, and Cairns, 1995; Cairns and others, 1995). Teacher-rated popularity was a composite of the items "popular with boys," "popular with girls," and "lots of friends," and teacher-rated aggression was a composite of the items "always argues," "gets in trouble," and "gets in fights." ICS-T scores were rated on seven-point Likert scales and were standardized within classroom and gender. Peer perceptions were gathered from limited-choice nomination items. Peer-assessed popularity was a single item measure, and peer nominations for aggression averaged three items: "starts fights," "gets in trouble," and "disruptive." Peer nominations were converted to proportions, transformed to approximate normality better, and standardized by sex. Then peer and teacher ratings were weighted equally in forming overall popularity and aggression composites. Liked-most nominations were only peer based and were also converted into standard scores within sex.

A series of one-way ANOVAs was conducted for girls and boys at the fourth-grade fall and spring assessments using the popularity composite (teacher and peer combined), peer, and the aggression composite (teacher and peer combined) as dependent variables and number of enemies as the independent variable with three levels: zero, one, and two/three (combined into one category). Table 5.4 presents the results. During the fall of fourth grade, boys with multiple enemies were less popular, less likable, and more aggressive than children with none or one enemy. Having enemies and being aggressive was positively related for girls, but having enemies was not related to popularity or likability. Differences between boys and girls flattened out for the spring. Both boys and girls with multiple enemies were

Table 5.4. Popularity, Likeability, and Aggression by Number of Enemies: Fall and Spring of Fourth Grade

	Popularity		Liked Most		Aggression	
	Girls	Boys	Girls	Boys	Girls	Boys
Fourth-grade fall enemies						
None	−.06 (0.98)	.08 (0.98)[a]	−.02 (1.05)	.08 (1.10)[a]	−.13 (1.00)[c]	−.23 (0.86)[b]
One	.14 (1.01)	.09 (1.05)[a]	.04 (0.88)	.10 (1.02)[a]	.21 (0.84)[b]	.20 (1.05)[b]
Two or three	.34 (1.12)	−.50 (0.87)[b]	.10 (0.77)	−.65 (0.68)[b]	.70 (1.09)[a]	.68 (1.14)[a]
F	0.59	4.72**	0.17	7.02**	7.24***	13.4***
Fourth-grade spring enemies						
None	.06 (0.97)[a]	.13 (0.99)[a]	.16 (0.95)[a]	.15 (1.10)[a]	−.19 (0.75)[b]	−.19 (0.90)[b]
One	.06 (1.04)[a]	.03 (0.93)[a]	.00 (0.93)[a,b]	−.01 (1.04)[a]	.03 (0.90)[b]	.03 (0.95)[b]
Two or three	−.47 (0.89)[b]	−.66 (1.02)[b]	−.44 (0.66)[b]	−.56 (0.57)[b]	1.16 (1.63)[a]	.57 (1.23)[a]
F	3.46*	8.47***	4.94**	6.28**	25.5***	7.96***

Note: All values are expressed in Z scores. SD's are in parentheses. For appropriate n's see Table 5.1. F's are (2,228) for boys and (2,246) for girls. Columns with different subscripts differ significantly from one another at the $p < .05$ level according to Tukey's honestly significant differences (HSD) post hoc test. Popularity and aggression measures are composites of ICS-T factors (POP and AGG) and peer nominations (popular and gets in fights/causes trouble/always argues). Liked-most measures are from peer nominations. *$p < .05$. **$p < .001$. ***$p < .001$.

less popular, less likable, and more aggressive than children with none or one enemy. Trends were similar when same- and opposite-sex enemies were considered. However, after controlling statistically for general peer dislike, having an enemy was uncorrelated with the Table 5.4 variables of perceived popularity, liked-most nominations, and aggression.

Our result differs from Abecassis and others (2002), who found statistically unique relations between having enemies and indicators of maladjustment. The discrepancy may be due to sample differences. There are five times as many children in the study by Abecassis and others (2002), giving them enviable power to reveal significant effects. The prevalence of mutual antipathies among their Dutch childhood sample was relatively low, possibly making the meaning of having an enemy different from when such relationships are common. If our power was indeed adequate, the failure of the Table 5.4 effects to survive the statistical controls of general peer dislike may imply that enemies are not for rejected children only. Although there is a mathematical dependence and a positive correlation between having an enemy and being generally disliked, boys and girls with enemies were both popular and unpopular, liked most by many and by few, and aggressive and nonaggressive. In short, children with mutual antipathies were pervasive in contributing to the normative peer cultures of middle childhood (see also Chapter Four, this volume).

Moreover, the fast-changing nature of enemy relationships may prevent all but a subset of the most severe, chronic cases of animosity from inflicting lasting damage on an individual. We attempted to take advantage of this fluidity by examining whether children who gained or lost enemies over the fourth grade showed consequent shifts in their popularity, or levels of aggression. A series of MLRs were performed with spring fourth-grade popularity, likability, and aggression as dependent variables. The independent variables were fall fourth-grade popularity, likability, or aggression, along with fall fourth-grade liked-least nominations (to control for general peer dislike) and an enemy change score (the difference of fall and spring) that ranged from −3 to +3. Results indicated that boys who lost same-sex enemies over the course of the school year became more popular [$t(227)$ = 2.00, r_p = −.13, $p < .05$] and less aggressive [$t(227)$ = 2.13, r_p = .14, $p < .05$]. An aggregate enemy change score showed similar effects, but effects for an opposite-sex change score were not significant. In contrast, girls who lost enemies, whether same or opposite sex, over the school year became more aggressive [$t(245)$ = 4.22, r_p = −.26, $p < .001$]. These results are not directly comparable to Abecassis and others (2002), who did not examine effects over this time span, but they support the contention that enemy relationships matter beyond the mere effects of peer dislike and are strongly contextualized by gender. A most interesting question for future research would be to replicate whether the loss of enemies over time leads to less aggressive behavior by boys but more aggressive behavior by girls.

Discussion

Our exploratory analysis of middle childhood antipathies suggests that relationships of dislike are common, often (but not always) of short duration, and partially reflective of the negative intergroup dynamics between boys and girls during the elementary school years. A substantial minority of children had one mutual antagonist, and a smaller minority had more than one. Fourth graders were more likely to be involved in mutual antipathies than third graders. Enemies tended to come and go. Fewer than one out of every five mutual antipathies recorded for the fall of fourth grade remained in the spring of fourth grade, and there was no association between the likelihood of having an antagonist between the third and fourth grades. However, even if specific enmity dyads tended to be of short duration, there was continuity in having (or not having) an antagonist of the same or opposite sex within the school year. Some children may be predisposed to engage in mutual feelings of negativity toward members of the same or opposite sex, at least within the confines of a particular social system. Children with multiple enemies were less popular and likable and more aggressive than children with none or one enemy, but these effects could not be differentiated from those of general peer dislike. However, even after controlling for peer dislike, boys who lost enemies over the school year became more popular and less aggressive, but girls who lost enemies became more aggressive.

One theme of our introductory comments was that an important body of work was lost in the time between the decline of peer research in the 1960s and its renaissance twenty years later with the ascendancy of rejection and risk paradigms. This older literature focused on childhood peer culture in the here-and-now, in addition to linking peer relationship processes with mental health and future adjustment (Adler and Adler, 1998). Of the new directions that the study of children's enemies can promote, we hope that among them is a renewed consideration of children's peer groups and social organizations (Cairns, Xie, and Leung, 1998; Cillessen and Bukowski, 2000). For example, children's mutual antipathies may be more useful as a dynamic indicator of the collective conflict (or lack thereof) between boy and girl peer cultures than a unique indicator of developmental risk (see also Chapter Six, this volume; Rodkin and Fischer, forthcoming). Or children's involvement in mutual antipathies may reveal themselves as a risk factor only under certain conditions, such as in interaction with community violence exposure (Chapter Three, this volume) or in connection with problematic parenting (Chapter Two, this volume). Consistent with our introductory review, our data are broadly in keeping with the notion that children's negative sentiments can reflect (and possibly anticipate) conflicts between children of different ethnic or socioeconomic backgrounds (Eder, Evans, and Parker, 1995; Mane, 1993), or a coordinated pattern of hostilities between children in peer groups whose norms and values conflict (Adler and Adler, 1998; Sherif, 1956), or whose interests coincide too closely. Patterns of animosity may also reflect an unequal power relationship between a bully and a victim and between included and excluded children (see Juvonen and Graham, 2001). For all these issues, research on children's antipathies might best be served by short-term longitudinal designs that capitalize on the dynamic nature of these relationships.

Another essential goal for future research on childhood antipathies is to clarify the phenomenology of enemy relations. In their analysis of friendships, Hartup and Stevens (1997) went beyond the question of whether children have a friend to examine the identity of one's friends and the qualitative properties, such as support, intimacy, and connectedness, that the friendship bond provides. Similar questions need to be asked of children's antipathies to go beyond the sparse, restrictive mathematical definition of mutual liked-least nominations. With whom is an inimical relationship developed: a boy or a girl; a peer of equal or unequal status; someone of the same or different ethnicity? What are the characteristics of the antipathy? How long does it endure? Do the participants withdraw from or attack one another? How did the antipathy originate? Is the antipathy a purely dyadic process or embedded in the classroom social network? A richer understanding of the variety of reasons that children can become antagonists is critical for progress in this emerging area of research.

References

Abecassis, M., and others. "Mutual Antipathies and Their Significance in Middle Childhood and Early Adolescence." *Child Development*, 2002, 73, 1543–1556.

Adler, P. A., and Adler, P. *Peer Power: Preadolescent Culture and Identity.* New Brunswick, N.J.: Rutgers University Press, 1998.

Asher, S. R., and Dodge, K. A. "Identifying Children Who Are Rejected by Their Peers." *Developmental Psychology*, 1986, 22, 444–449.

Benenson, J. F., and others. "The Influence of Group Size on Children's Competitive Behavior." *Child Development*, 2001, 72, 921–928.

Cairns, R. B., and Cairns, B. D. *Lifelines and Risks*. London: Harvester, 1994.

Cairns, R. B., Leung, M-C., Buchanan, L., and Cairns, B. D. "Friendships and Social Networks in Childhood and Adolescence: Fluidity, Reliability, and Interrelations." *Child Development*, 1995, 66, 1330–1345.

Cairns, R. B., Leung, M-C., Gest, S. D., and Cairns, B. D. "A Brief Method for Assessing Social Development: Structure, Reliability, Stability, and Developmental Validity of the Interpersonal Competence Scale." *Behavioral Research and Therapy*, 1995, 33, 725–736.

Cairns, R. B., Xie, H., and Leung, M-C. "The Popularity of Friendships and the Neglect of Social Networks: Towards a New Balance." In W. M. Bukowski and A. H. Cillessen (eds.), *Sociometry Then and Now: Building on Six Decades of Measuring Experiences with the Peer Group*. New Directions for Child Development, no. 80. San Francisco: Jossey-Bass, 1998.

Cillessen, A.H.N., and Bukowski, W. M. "Conceptualizing and Measuring Peer Acceptance and Rejection." In A.H.N. Cillessen and W. M. Bukowski (eds.), *Recent Advances in the Measurement of Acceptance and Rejection in the Peer System*. New Directions for Child Development, no. 88. San Francisco: Jossey-Bass, 2000.

Clark, K. B., and Clark, M. P. "Racial Identification and Preference in Negro Children." In T. M. Newcomb and E. L. Hartley (eds.), *Readings in Social Psychology*. New York: Holt, 1947.

Coie, J. D., Dodge, K. A., and Coppotelli, H. "Dimensions and Types of Social Status: A Cross-Age Perspective." *Developmental Psychology*, 1982, 18, 557–570.

Cooley, C. H. *Human Nature and the Social Order*. (Rev. ed.) New York: Scribner, 1922.

Eder, D., Evans, C. C., and Parker, S. *School Talk: Gender and Adolescent Culture*. New Brunswick, N.J.: Rutgers University Press, 1995.

Frude, N. "Hatred Between Children." In V. Varna (ed.), *How and Why Children Hate*. London: Jessica Kingsley, 1993.

Gronlund, N. E. *Sociometry in the Classroom*. New York: HarperCollins, 1959.

Hartup, W. W., and Stevens, N. "Friendships and Adaptation in the Life Course." *Psychological Bulletin*, 1997, 121, 355–370.

Haselager, G.J.T., Hartup, W. W., van Lieshout, C.F.M., and Riksen-Walraven, J.M.A. "Similarities Between Friends and Nonfriends in Middle Childhood." *Child Development*, 1998, 69, 1198–1208.

Hayes, D. S., Gershman, E., and Bolin, L. J. "Friends and Enemies: Cognitive Bases for Preschool Children's Unilateral and Reciprocal Relationships." *Child Development*, 1980, 51, 1276–1279.

Heider, F. *The Psychology of Interpersonal Relations*. New York: Wiley, 1958.

Homans, G. C. *Social Behavior: Its Elementary Forms*. New York: Harcourt Brace, 1961.

Juvonen, J., and Graham, S. (eds.). *Peer Harassment in School: The Plight of the Vulnerable and Victimized*. New York: Guilford Press, 2001.

Ladd, B. K., and Ladd, G. W. "Variations in Peer Victimization: Relations to Children's Maladjustment." In J. Juvonen and S. Graham (eds.), *Peer Harassment in School: The Plight of the Vulnerable and Victimized*. New York: Guilford Press, 2001.

Maccoby, E. E. *The Two Sexes: Growing Up Apart, Coming Together*. Cambridge, Mass.: Harvard University Press, 1998.

Mane, N. "Children and Hate: Hostility Caused by Racial Prejudice." In V. Varna (ed.), *How and Why Children Hate*. London: Jessica Kingsley, 1993.

Martin, C. L., and Fabes, R. A. "The Stability and Consequences of Young Children's Same-Sex Peer Interactions." *Developmental Psychology*, 2001, 37, 431–446.

Moreno, J. L. *Who Shall Survive: A New Approach to the Study of Human Interrelations*. Washington, D.C.: Nervous and Mental Disease Publishing Co., 1934.

Moreno, J. L. "Sociometry and the Cultural Order." *Sociometry Monographs*, 1943, 2, 299–344.

Rodkin, P. C., and Fischer, K. "Sexual Harassment and the Cultures of Childhood: Psychological and Legal Perspectives." *Journal of Applied School Psychology*, forthcoming.

Schneider, B. H. *Friends and Enemies: Peer Relations in Childhood.* New York: Oxford University Press, 2001.

Sherif, M. "Experiments in Group Conflict." *Scientific American*, 1956, *195*, 54–58.

Sullivan, H. S. *The Interpersonal Theory of Psychiatry* (H. S. Perry and M. L. Gawel, eds.). New York: Norton, 1953.

Thorne, B. *Gender Play: Girls and Boys in School.* New Brunswick, N.J.: Rutgers University Press, 1993.

Underwood, M. K., Schockner, A. E., and Hurley, J. C. "Children's Responses to Same- and Other-Gender Peers: An Experimental Investigation with Eight-, Ten-, and Twelve-Year-Olds." *Developmental Psychology*, 2001, *37*, 362–372.

Vaughn, B. E., and others. "Dyadic Analyses of Friendship in a Sample of Preschool-Age Children Attending Head Start: Correspondence Between Measures and Implications for Social Competence." *Child Development*, 2001, *72*, 862–878.

PHILIP C. RODKIN *is assistant professor in the department of educational psychology at the University of Illinois at Urbana-Champaign.*

RUTH PEARL *is professor in the department of educational psychology at the University of Illinois at Chicago.*

THOMAS W. FARMER *is associate director of the Center for Developmental Science and research associate professor in education and psychology at the University of North Carolina at Chapel Hill.*

RICHARD VAN ACKER *is professor in the department of special education at the University of Illinois at Chicago.*

6

The concurrent and longitudinal risk of enemy relationships, using both nominations- and ratings-based methods of assessing enmity, were examined among elementary school children. After controlling for peer rejection, only ratings-based enemies were found to have negative developmental impact.

Developmental Risk Associated with Mutual Dislike in Elementary School Children

Alice W. Pope

The developmental risk of childhood peer rejection—being disliked—has been well documented. Surprisingly, although relationships involving mutual liking (friendships) have received extensive attention, investigations regarding mutual dislike are few (Hartup and Abecassis, 2002). Mutual dislike may be a common occurrence in middle childhood; in one sample of eight year olds, 65 percent had at least one same-sex mutual antipathy, as defined by concordant negative nominations (Hembree and Vandell, 2000). An important question is whether the phenomenon of mutual dislike is associated with adjustment and whether the risk of adjustment problems differs from that associated with simply being the recipient of peer dislike (that is, rejection). Preliminary investigations indicate that mutual antipathies, distinct from peer rejection, are associated with problematic social and academic adjustment (Hembree and Vandell, 2000) and with aggression, social ineffectiveness, and bullying (Abecassis and others, 2002) in elementary school children.

There is reason to expect that having enemies would be associated with adjustment in children. Presumably, enemy relationships are conflictual, hostile, and a source of ongoing unpleasantness. Some children might become anxious and withdrawn as a result of wanting to avoid their enemies; others could develop exacerbated aggressive behavior, as they are repeatedly angered by encounters with the disliked partner. Alternatively, aspects of adjustment could themselves influence the likelihood that some

NEW DIRECTIONS FOR CHILD AND ADOLESCENT DEVELOPMENT, no. 102, Winter 2003   © Wiley Periodicals, Inc.

children would develop enemy relationships. For example, aggressive, over-active, and immature behaviors might lead to unilateral rejection early on (Pope and Bierman, 1999) and later lead to reciprocal enmity due to the rejected children's anger and frustration at those excluding them.

The purpose of the study examined in this chapter was to contribute to the nascent study of enemy relationships by assessing the risk of concurrent and future adjustment problems among children experiencing mutual dislike.

Method

The year 1 sample consisted of 413 children (51 percent girls; 8 percent black, 37 percent Hispanic, 54 percent Anglo) in grades 3 through 6 in a small south-western city. Participants were distributed across twenty-nine classrooms in four schools (mean participants per classroom = 14). Classroom peer group acceptance was evaluated using liked-most and liked-least nominations (nom-inations were limited to three) and a five-point likability rating scale, where children were asked to indicate how much they liked to play with each class-mate. Social adjustment was evaluated using classroom peer nominations of single-item variables: aggressive ("say they can beat everybody up"), overac-tive ("out of their seat a lot"), withdrawn ("aren't noticed much"), immature ("act like a baby"), sad ("sad"), anxious ("worry a lot"), and helpful ("help oth-ers"). All procedures allowed for both same-sex and cross-sex nominations or ratings. In year 2, 67 percent (n = 213) of the year 1 grades 3 through 5 sam-ple, now in grades 4 through 6, was reassessed using identical measures. Attrition analyses showed that children lost to follow-up were lower in lika-bility and helpfulness; no other differences were found. All variables were stan-dardized within grade and gender. Social Preference (standardized liked-most nominations minus standardized liked-least nominations) and Social Impact (standardized liked-most nominations plus standardized liked-least nomina-tions) were calculated according to the Coie, Dodge, and Coppotelli (1982) procedures.

Results

Children with mutual dislike relationships were identified using two meth-ods, and these methods were contrasted in the examination of concurrent and longitudinal adjustment variables.

Defining Enemy Relationships. In this sample, peer acceptance was measured using both nominations and rating scale measures. Dislike, or rejection, is most commonly assessed using dislike nominations. However, the use of rating scales has a long history in the assessment of children's preferences regarding peers and has some advantages over nominations. Some have argued that ratings are more reliable than nominations (Asher and Hymel, 1981). Certainly, ratings ensure that all participating classmates are considered, whereas nominations depend to a greater extent on children's ability to remember and identify classmates who are most salient for liking and disliking. Although ratings are often used to derive a mean score reflecting the average level of acceptance by peers, the end points can be validly used as equivalents to liked-most and liked-least nominations (Bukowski, Sippola, Hoza, and Newcomb, 2000). Using the lowest rating of likability ("not at all") as a means to identify mutual dislike would have the advantage of providing the opportunity for more than three mutual dislike relationships. Also, using ratings rather than nominations might result in greater distinction between the enemy variable and dislike nominations, so that the possibility of identifying predictive variance unique to enemy relationships would be improved. Therefore, enemy relationships were defined in this study in two ways in order to contrast the more commonly used approach—mutual negative nominations—with a means that permits unlimited choices, mutual ratings of "not at all liked." The correlation between the two types of enemy scores (calculated as the raw frequencies of mutual dislike pairings) was .33, more modest than might be expected. A frequency table revealed that only 39 percent of the children with zero on nominations-based enemy scores also had zero enemies as derived from ratings. In fact, children with zero enemies on the nominations score had up to six enemies on the ratings-based enemy score.

Incidence of Mutual Dislike. For descriptive purposes and to compare with other studies, the incidence of mutual dislike relationships is reported with both nominations- and ratings-based methods.

Nominations-Based Enemy Relationships. Of the year 1 sample, 33 percent had one or more enemies (the range was zero to three, given the limited-choice negative nominations). Approximately two-thirds of the sample had no mutual negative nominations; zero was both the mode and the median for number of enemies. The incidence of enemy relationships found here differs substantially from the rates reported by Hembree and Vandell (2000) for their sample of eight year olds, where they found twice the rate (65 percent) of children with enemies, using mutual negative nominations.

Table 6.1 shows percentages of children with and without enemies, by grade level, gender, and ethnicity. No gender or ethnicity differences were found, but chi-square analyses indicated a higher incidence of having one or more enemies for older (grades 5 through 6; 38 percent) than younger (grades 3 and 4; 28 percent) children [$\chi^2(1) = 4.66, p < .03$].

It might be expected that children in various sociometric classification groups would vary in their likelihood of having enemy relationships. In this sample, 13 percent of popular children, 31 percent of average children, 53 percent of controversial children, 40 percent of neglected children, and 60 percent of rejected children had at least one enemy (classification made here using the procedures of Coie, Dodge, and Coppotelli, 1982). Statistical differences were found between popular and average [$\chi^2(1) = 7.47, p < .05$] and average and rejected groups [$\chi^2(1) = 15.43, p < .0001$]; popular children were not contrasted with any group other than average. Not surprisingly, these rates are lower than those reported by Hembree and Vandell (2000), who found a larger overall incidence of enemy relationships and, consequently, higher rates in each sociometric category. The rates in the current sample are roughly half of what was previously reported, with the exception of the neglected group, which was the same (Hembree and Vandell, 2000). In keeping with the usual conceptualization of rejected and controversial status, it makes sense that over half of the children in these two groups would experience relationships characterized by mutual dislike; indeed, it might be expected that this rate would be even higher. Somewhat surprising is the finding that even popular children can have enemy relationships. Perhaps the most unexpected finding is that almost half of the neglected children, who would be expected to make a minimal impression on peers, were involved in mutual dislike relationships.

Ratings-Based Enemy Relationships. Using mutual likability ratings of 1 to define mutual dislike (enemies), 67 percent of children had at least one enemy—double the rate found through the use of nominations to derive the enemy variable. The range was 0 to 11; the median was 1, and the mode was 0. Incidence rates by grade level, gender, and ethnicity are reported in Table 6.1. Across all demographic groups, it was more common to have an enemy than not. Older children were significantly more likely to have enemies than younger children $[\chi^2(1) = 3.95, p < .05]$, but boys and girls were equally likely to have enemies. In comparisons of the ethnicity groups, Anglo children were more likely to have enemies than were Hispanic children $[\chi^2(1) = 8.14, p < .005]$.

Table 6.1. Proportion of Children Within Demographic Groups with and Without Enemies

Demographic Variables	Number of Enemies (Nominations)		Number of Enemies (Ratings)	
	None	One or More	None	One or More
Grades				
3 and 4	72	28	37	63
5 and 6	62	38	29	71
Gender				
Boys	65	35	32	68
Girls	69	31	34	66
Ethnicity				
Anglo	64	36	27	73
Black	59	41	34	66
Hispanic	73	27	42	58

Note: Numbers are row-wise percentages, calculated separately for each method of defining enemy variable (using like-least nominations versus likeability ratings).

Within the sociometric classifications, at least one enemy was present for 54 percent of popular children, 66 percent of average children, 80 percent of controversial children, 90 percent of neglected children, and 86 percent of rejected children. Only the rejected and average groups differed significantly in number of enemy relationships [$\chi^2(1) = 6.43, p < .01$] (the popular group was compared only with the average group, and these were not significantly different). When children were not limited in the number of classmates whom they could rate as disliked, having an enemy relationship was quite common even for well-liked children; for those typically thought of as having problematic peer relationships, having an enemy relationship was almost universal.

Dislike Versus Mutual Dislike: Redundant Information? Extensive research has demonstrated that children who are disliked by classmates tend to experience a range of adjustment problems. An important question, then, is whether having enemies provides any further predictability beyond what would be expected by being the subject of unidirectional dislike by the group.

Negative nominations and number of enemies correlated significantly but not perfectly ($r = .49$ for nominations-based enemies, $r = .28$ for ratings-based enemies), indicating that being disliked by peers does not inevitably involve mutual dislike. Of the sixty-two children classified as peer rejected in year 1, 40 percent had no enemies using the nominations method. Using the ratings method, where having enemies was more common than not, there was still a substantial group of rejected children without a single enemy (15 percent). Having enemies does not appear to be synonymous with sociometrically derived rejected status or even with being generally disliked.

Enemy Relationships and Adjustment: Analysis Strategy. The association between number of enemies and adjustment was evaluated both concurrently and longitudinally (using enemies in the first year to predict adjustment in the second year). The first test of association was to inspect correlations between number of enemies and the adjustment variables; for the concurrent analyses, Pearson correlations were used, and for the longitudinal analyses, semipartial correlations were used, covarying year 1 levels of adjustment. The second strategy was to conduct multiple regressions, entering number of enemies simultaneously with negative nominations, to determine whether enemy relationships contributed unique variance, beyond that of being unilaterally disliked, to predict adjustment (for the longitudinal analyses, year 1 level of adjustment was entered first). Finally, in the instances where neither enemies nor negative nominations contributed significant independent variance to the prediction of adjustment, the block of enemies plus negative nominations was inspected to see if the two variables together made a significant contribution. Parallel analyses were conducted throughout for enemies scores derived from nominations and from ratings. All correlations and semipartial correlations reported are significant at $p < .05$; although this is a fairly liberal standard given the number of analyses conducted, it was deemed appropriate to be lenient given the exploratory nature of this work.

Concurrent Risk. The concurrent association between enemy relationships and adjustment was examined for both nominations- and ratings-based methods.

Nominations-Based Enemy Relationships. Number of enemy relationships was significantly correlated with all adjustment variables except anxious (see Table 6.2). However, when examining the independent variance contributed by enemies when dislike nominations were simultaneously entered into the prediction (regression 1 in Table 6.2), only dislike nominations predicted concurrent adjustment (the only exception being a small but significant semipartial correlation between number of enemies and sadness). This suggests that any concurrent association between having enemies and social adjustment is most likely due to the level of unidirectional dislike.

Ratings-Based Enemy Relationships. The enemies variable was correlated with seven of ten of the adjustment variables (see Table 6.2). In the multiple regressions (regression 2 in Table 6.2), enemies also provided statistically significant independent variance in the prediction of most of the adjustment variables, while dislike nominations contributed uniquely to all ten.

Future Risk. The longitudinal association between early enemy relationships and later adjustment was examined for both nominations- and ratings-based methods.

Nominations-Based Enemy Relationships. The semipartial correlations between number of enemies and adjustment variables (with year 1 levels of adjustment controlled) showed no significant associations (see Table 6.3). The semipartial correlations showed that number of enemies did not predict social adjustment one year later, beyond the effects of earlier dislike.

Ratings-Based Enemy Relationships. Here, too, enemies failed to predict adjustment the following year, as seen in the semipartial correlations in Table 6.3. Similarly, in the multiple regressions, the enemy variable made no independent contribution to predicting adjustment; semipartial correlations were all close to zero, even while dislike nominations provided incremental variance to the prediction of four of the ten adjustment variables (see Table 6.3). These results suggest that having enemies does not itself increase the likelihood of adjustment problems a year later, whereas being the target of dislike (regardless of reciprocation) does.

Summary. Ratings-based enemies scores provided substantially more predictive utility than did nominations-based scores, which showed associations with adjustment only through variance shared with dislike nominations. However, ratings-based enemies were independently related only to concurrent adjustment problems; neither type of enemies scores predicted adjustment the following year.

Table 6.2. Concurrent Bivariate and Semipartial Correlations Between Adjustment and Number of Enemies and Dislike Nominations

Adjustment Variable	r Number of Enemies (Nominations)	r Number of Enemies (Ratings)	r Dislike Nominations	Regression 1		Regression 2	
				sr Number of Enemies (Nominations)	sr Dislike Nominations	sr Number of Enemies (Ratings)	sr Dislike Nominations
Social Preference	−.40***	−.35**	−.82***	−.02	−.70***	−.09**	−.74***
Social Impact	.28***	.06	.60***	−.10	.53***	−.13**	.60***
Likeability	−.32**	−.50***	−.58**	−.03	−.49**	−.33***	−.44***
Anxious	.05	.08	.16**	−.03	.16**	.04	.10*
Helpful	−.19**	−.22***	−.38**	−.00	−.33**	−.11*	−.31***
Withdrawn	.25**	.29***	.53**	−.01	.46**	.12**	.46***
Immature	.27**	.27***	.57***	−.00	.51**	.09*	.51***
Aggressive	.24***	−.02	.37***	.06	−.30**	−.15**	.39***
Sad	.12*	.16**	.42**	−.09*	.41**	.03	.37***
Overactive	.18**	.12*	.38**	−.00	.33**	.00	.35***

Note: Regression 1 involved simultaneously entering number of enemies (calculated using dislike nominations) and standardized dislike nominations. Regression 2 involved simultaneously entering number of enemies (calculated using likeability ratings) and standardized dislike nominations. $n = 413$. $*p < .05$; $**p < .005$; $***p < .0005$.

Table 6.3. Semipartial Correlations Between Year 2 Adjustment and Year 1 Number of Enemies and Dislike Nominations

Adjustment Variable	r Number of Enemies (Nominations)[a]	r Number of Enemies (Ratings)[a]	r Dislike Nominations[a]	Regression 1		Regression 2	
				sr Number of Enemies (Nominations)	sr Dislike Nominations	sr Number of Enemies (Ratings)	sr Dislike Nominations
Social Preference	.03	−.01	−.10	.06	−.11*	.00	−.09
Social Impact	−.08	.03	.04	−.10	.08	.03	.02
Likeability	.04	.06	−.18**	.04	−.18**	.05	−.19***
Anxious	−.01	.02	.02	−.02	.03	.01	.01
Helpful	−.09	−.06	−.22***	.02	−.20***	.01	−.21***
Withdrawn	−.01	.11	.13*	−.08	.15*	.08	.11
Immature	.02	.01	.14*	−.04	.15*	−.02	.14*
Aggressive	−.04	.01	.10	−.09	.12*	−.03	.09
Sad	.05	.05	.09	.00	.08	.02	.08
Overactive	.04	.01	.19**	−.05	.19**	−.05	.19**

Note: Regression 1 involved simultaneously entering number of enemies (calculated using dislike nominations) and standardized dislike nominations. Regression 2 involved simultaneously entering number of enemies (calculated using likeability ratings) and standardized dislike nominations. For both regressions, year 1 levels of the adjustment variable were controlled. $n = 213$. $*p < .05$; $**p < .005$; $***p < .0005$.

[a]Semipartial correlation with Year 1 level of adjustment variable controlled.

Context and Mutual Dislike

Increasingly, researchers are recognizing the importance of context in understanding children's peer relationships. Gender, culture, and even the social environment particular to individual schools all have the potential to shift the way that children's social behaviors are interpreted by peers (Hartup, 1983; Rubin, Bukowski, and Parker, 1998). It may be that the presence of enemy relationships becomes more meaningful within certain contexts. With this in mind, some exploratory analyses were conducted to examine the possibility that enemy relationships may be uniquely related to adjustment in specific contexts.

Gender. Because the correlates of peer acceptance seem to differ for school-age boys and girls, along with preferred activities and type of social networks (Bierman and Welsh, 1997), it may be that the presence of enemy relationships bears different associations with adjustment depending on the gender of the child. To explore this possibility, correlations and multiple regressions were conducted as before, examining the strength of association between enemies scores (based on nominations and ratings) and adjustment at year 1 and year 2.

Nominations-Based Enemy Relationships. Correlations between enemies scores and concurrent (year 1) adjustment were significant for almost all adjustment variables, with the exception of anxious for both boys and girls and sad for boys (rs ranging from $\pm.15$ to .47). When considered together with dislike nominations in multiple regression analyses, enemy relationships made no incremental prediction beyond that of dislike. For girls, semi-partial correlations ranged from $-.09$ to .10, with none reaching statistical significance. For boys, significant variance was contributed by number of enemies for the prediction of year 1 likability ($sr = -.14$) and aggression ($sr = .14$).

In the prediction of year 2 adjustment (with year 1 adjustment controlled), enemies scores were not significantly correlated with any adjustment variable for boys or for girls. In multiple regressions, enemies scores contributed no incremental variance beyond that of dislike nominations to predict adjustment for girls, but for boys, enemies scores predicted decreases in withdrawal ($sr = -.16$). In addition, for boys, the block of enemies plus dislike nominations significantly predicted increased overactivity [$\delta R^2 = .05$; $F(2,103) = 3.53$, $p < .05$], although neither predictor provided independent prediction.

Ratings-Based Enemy Relationships. In year 1, boys' enemies scores were significantly and negatively correlated with social preference, likability ratings, and helpfulness and positively correlated with withdrawal and immaturity (rs ranging from $\delta.21$ to .50). Girls' enemies scores showed the same pattern of correlations, and in addition were correlated with sadness (rs ranging from $\delta.21$ to .51). In multiple regressions, enemies scores were significant independent predictors of low levels of social preference and likability ratings, for both boys ($sr = -.10$ and $-.34$, respectively) and girls ($sr = -.09$ and $-.32$, respectively). In addition, enemies scores showed significant independent variance in predicting low social impact for boys ($sr = -.14$) and, for girls, withdrawal and low aggression ($sr = .15$ and $-.23$, respectively).

In the longitudinal analyses (with year 1 levels controlled), enemies scores were not correlated with any of the second-year adjustment variables, with the exception of an increase in withdrawal for girls only ($sr = .24$). However, in multiple regressions, enemies contributed significant independent variance beyond that of dislike nominations to predict increased likability for boys ($sr = .16$) and increased withdrawal for girls ($sr = .20$). In addition, for boys, the combined contribution of enemies plus dislike nominations significantly predicted overactivity [$\delta R^2 = .06$, $F(2, 103) = 4.29$, $p < .05$].

Summary. Nominations-based enemies were significant independent predictors for only two adjustment variables out of forty analyses (boys and girls, at year 1 and year 2). In contrast, ratings-based enemies scores showed more correspondence with adjustment, including negative concurrent associations with both measures of peer acceptance (social preference and likability), beyond the effects of dislike nominations. Interestingly, for girls, ratings-based enemies also showed independent prediction of withdrawal, concurrently as well as longitudinally, as well as a negative relationship with aggression.

Same- Versus Mixed-Sex Enemy Relationships. Perhaps a more meaningful way of conceptualizing enemy relationships in terms of gender is to examine same-sex and opposite-sex pairs. Because school-age children prefer same-sex peers (Maccoby and Jacklin, 1987) and have more positive feelings and trust in same-sex peers (Rotenberg, 1986), same-sex enemy relationships might be particularly hurtful and damaging to adjustment. This might be particularly true for girls, who tend to have fewer, but more intimate, friendships than do boys (Eder and Hallinan, 1978). Mixed-sex enemy relationships might be expected to have less impact on adjustment during the elementary school years, because children commonly avoid opposite-sex peers and appear to expect to be hurt by them more often than by their own sex (Powlishta, Serbin, Doyle, and White, 1994). In contrast to these conceptually based predictions, Abecassis and others (2002) found that mixed-sex enemy relationships were associated with more problematic adjustment in girls than in boys.

In terms of prevalence rates, using nominations-based scores, 17 percent had same-sex enemies only, 14 percent had mixed-sex only, and 3 percent had both types of enemy relationships. It was more common to have either same-sex [$\chi^2(1) = 42.98$, $p < .0001$] or mixed-sex [$\chi^2(1) = 30.22$, $p < .0001$] than both types of enemy relationships. For ratings-based enemy scores, 7 percent of children with enemies had only same-sex enemies, 43 percent had only mixed-sex enemies, and 12 percent had both types. Mixed-sex and both types of enemy relationships were more common than having only same-sex enemies [$\chi^2(1)$ = 106.22, p < .0001 and $\chi^2(1)$ = 4.57, p < .05, respectively]. In addition, mixed-sex enemies relationships were more common than having both types [$\chi^2(1)$ = 74.12, p < .0001]. For both ratings and nominations, there were no significant gender differences in rates of enemy type.

Nominations-Based Enemy Relationships. For girls, same-sex enemy relationships were concurrently correlated with low social preference and with social impact, withdrawal, and immaturity (rs ranging from ±.15 to .18). Girls with mixed-sex enemy relationships showed the same pattern of associations with adjustment variables; in addition, significant correlations were seen with sadness, overactivity, and low likability ratings (rs ranging from ±.14 to .30). For boys, same-sex enemy relationships were negatively correlated with positive adjustment (social preference, likability ratings, and helpfulness) and positively correlated with withdrawal, immaturity, aggression, and overactivity (rs ranging from ±.10 to .31). In contrast, mixed-sex enemy relationships were correlated only with social impact and aggression, and negatively correlated with social preference and likability ratings (rs ranging from ±.20 to .33). When same-sex and mixed-sex enemies scores were entered into a multiple regression along with dislike nominations, neither type of enemy score contributed significant independent variance in predicting year 1 adjustment for girls; however, for boys, same-sex enemies independently predicted low likability ratings (sr = ±.12), and mixed-sex enemies independently predicted aggression (sr = .13).

In the longitudinal analyses (with year 1 levels controlled), girls' same-sex enemies did not correlate with any adjustment variables, while mixed-sex enemies scores were negatively correlated with likability ratings and helpfulness (sr = −.18 and −.17, respectively) . Boys' same-sex enemies were negatively correlated with withdrawal (sr = −.19), but mixed-sex enemies scores were not significant predictors of year 2 adjustment. When the two types of enemies scores were entered into multiple regressions along with dislike nominations, neither enemies score was a significant independent predictor of year 2 adjustment for girls, while only same-sex enemies provided significant incremental variance in predicting decreased withdrawal for boys (sr = −.19).

Ratings-Based Enemy Relationships. For girls, same-sex enemies were positively correlated with year 1 social impact, withdrawal, and aggression and negatively correlated with social preference and likability (rs ranging from ±.16 to .22). Mixed-sex enemies were positively correlated with withdrawal, immaturity, and sadness and negatively correlated with social preference, likability, helpfulness, and aggression (rs ranging from ±.17 to .47). When the two types of enemy relationships were considered together with dislike nominations, same-sex enemies did not contribute significant independent variance to the prediction of concurrent adjustment. In contrast, mixed-sex enemies were independently significant in the prediction of social preference ($sr = -.10$), social impact ($sr = -.13$), likability ($sr = -.33$), withdrawal ($sr = .14$), and aggression ($sr = -.27$). Examining associations between enemies relationships and year 2 adjustment (with year 1 adjustment controlled), the only significant correlation was mixed-sex enemies predicting increases in withdrawal ($sr = .26$). The identical pattern held when the two types of enemies scores were entered into multiple regressions together with dislike nominations; the only enemy variable to contribute significant incremental variance was mixed-sex enemies predicting year 2 withdrawal ($sr = -.16$).

For boys, same-sex enemies were positively correlated with year 1 withdrawal, immaturity, and overactivity and negatively correlated with social preference and likability. Mixed-sex enemies were negatively correlated with social preference, likability, and helpfulness and positively correlated with withdrawal and immaturity. In multiple regressions, where both types of enemies scores were considered along with dislike nominations, the only significant independent contributions made by enemies variables were same-sex enemies predicting social impact ($sr = -.11$) and both same-sex and mixed-sex enemies predicting likability ($sr = -.12$ and $-.30$, respectively) and mixed-sex enemies predicting aggression ($sr = .13$). In the longitudinal analyses (with year 1 levels of adjustment controlled), neither same-sex nor mixed-sex enemies scores correlated significantly with year 2 adjustment variables. When the two types of enemies scores were entered into multiple regressions together with dislike nominations, the only significant independent contribution made by enemies scores was same-sex enemies predicting year 2 decreases in withdrawal ($sr = -.16$).

Summary. For both nominations and ratings, same-sex enemies scores for boys provided independent prediction of concurrent low likability, as well as decreasing withdrawal the following year. Using ratings-based scores, mixed-sex (but not same-sex) enemies for girls showed independent associations with adjustment on half of the concurrent variables. Interestingly, however, the associations were not consistently in a problematic direction. Although girls with mixed-sex enemies were lower on social preference and likability and higher on withdrawal, they were also lower on aggression. Nominations-based same-sex and mixed-sex enemies were uninformative for girls.

Ethnicity and Culture. There is little previous work to guide hypotheses related to differences in the form and meaning of peer relations across cultures (Rubin, Bukowski, and Parker, 1998). Our sample allows exploration of this issue through having sizable numbers of both Anglo and Hispanic participants and because of a naturalistic experiment of sorts, in that two of the participating schools were single ethnicity (one Anglo and one Hispanic) and two were mixed.

In what ways might enemy relationships be differentially related to adjustment, depending on ethnicity? The Hispanic population of this city was almost entirely Mexican, and many families were fairly recent immigrants who would be expected to be continuing many of their cultural traditions. Essentially, no empirical work exists describing culture-specific aspects of peer relations of Mexican American children. However, family systems theory, which attends closely to cultural issues, notes that family relationships are preeminent in Mexican American society, to the point where it is common for parents to encourage children to prioritize siblings and cousins as primary peer relationships and to downplay relationships with unrelated children (Falicov, 1982). In this context, enemy relationships among classmates might be expected to be of little concern to Mexican American children. In contrast, Anglo children, who are expected to form and maintain relationships with peers at school, might be greatly affected by mutual dislike. To examine these issues, separate analyses were conducted for a school with all Hispanic children, n = 51; a school with all Anglo children, n = 92; and two schools with Anglo, Hispanic, and black children, n = 263.

Nominations-Based Enemy Relationships. In the Hispanic school, correlations between number of enemy relationships and adjustment variables were all nonsignificant in year 1. Enemies scores did not contribute significant independent variance in concurrent prediction of adjustment variables, beyond that of negative nominations, in regression equations. There were no significant correlations between year 1 enemies scores and year 2 adjustment (with year 1 adjustment covaried), except for a negative correlation with likability ratings. Again, enemies did not contribute significant independent variance at year 2.

For the Anglo school, enemies scores were significantly correlated with problematic adjustment on all year 1 variables except worried (rs ranging from ±.22 to .48). However, these significant relations were due to the variance shared with dislike nominations, as demonstrated in the multiple regressions, where only dislike nominations contributed significant incremental prediction to concurrent adjustment. When year 2 adjustment was considered, only sadness was significantly predicted by enemies scores the year before (sr = .36). This relationship held even when enemies scores were simultaneously entered into multiple regressions with dislike nominations, as enemies contributed significant independent variance (sr = .32).

In the mixed-ethnicity schools, enemies scores were concurrently correlated with social impact, withdrawal, immaturity, and aggression and with low levels of social preference, likability ratings, and helpfulness (rs ranging from ±.19 to .44). In the multiple regressions, although dislike nominations provided significant independent variance for all adjustment variables (except anxiety), enemies did so only for low levels of sadness (sr = −.12). In predicting later adjustment (with initial levels of adjustment controlled), enemies showed no significant correlations. On the multiple regressions including dislike nominations, however, having enemies independently predicted decreasing aggression (sr = −.18) and sadness (sr = −.17) a year later.

Ratings-Based Enemy Relationships. In the Hispanic school, enemies were significantly correlated with concurrent withdrawal and immaturity and with low levels of social preference, likability, and helpfulness (rs ranging from ±.30 to .50). Enemies scores provided significant independent prediction beyond that of dislike nominations in concurrently predicting withdrawal and low likability (sr = .34 and −.57, respectively). Enemies did not, however, show any significant association with adjustment at year 2; with initial levels of adjustment controlled, enemies scores were not correlated with adjustment and did not provide significant independent variance in the multiple regression with dislike nominations.

In the Anglo school, enemies scores were significantly correlated with year 1 withdrawal, immaturity, sadness, and overactivity, and they were negatively correlated with social preference, likability, and helpfulness (rs ranging from ±.26 to .57). In multiple regressions, enemies contributed significant independent variance, beyond the contribution of dislike nominations, to predict problematic adjustment in terms of likability (sr = −.36), helpfulness (sr = −.32), and withdrawal (sr = .18). When predicting year 2 adjustment, enemies correlated significantly only with increased withdrawal (sr = .23); neither enemies nor dislike nominations contributed significant independent variance to predicting year 2 adjustment, although the block of both variables together significantly predicted low levels of social preference [δR^2 = .11, $F(2,49)$ = 5.99, p < .01] and likability [δR^2 = .06, $F(2,49)$ = 4.20, p < .05].

In the mixed-ethnicity school, enemies were significantly correlated with concurrent withdrawal, immaturity, and sadness, as well as low levels of social preference, likability, and helpfulness (rs ranging from ±.14 to .46). In multiple regressions, enemies provided significant incremental variance beyond that of dislike nominations to predict social preference, social impact, likability, and aggression, all in a negative direction (sr = −.08, −.12, −.29, and −.15, respectively). These associations did not extend into the second year, however, as there were no significant relationships between enemies and year 2 adjustment.

Summary. There was little correspondence in the pattern of associations seen for nominations-based versus ratings-based enemies in this set of analyses. There were fewest independent associations with adjustment, for either method of deriving enemies scores, for the Hispanic school and most independent associations with adjustment for the mixed ethnicity school. Interestingly, of the four significant independent associations seen for nominations-based enemies, three were in the direction of positive adjustment, all for the mixed-ethnicity school (negative semipartial correlations with concurrent and future sadness, as well as negative semipartial correlation with future aggression).

Same-Ethnicity and Cross-Ethnicity Enemy Relationships. Another way of considering the role of ethnicity is to examine same- versus cross-ethnicity mutual dislike pairings. It may be that same-ethnicity enemy relationships would be more detrimental to adjustment than cross-ethnicity enmities, because there can be less expectation of harmonious relationships across ethnic lines (Hartup, 1983). Accordingly, the association between these two types of enemy relationships and adjustment was examined. When multiple regressions were conducted, same-ethnicity enemies, cross-ethnicity enemies, and standardized dislike nominations were entered simultaneously to determine independent effects of each type of enemy relationships, over and above the effects of group-level dislike. Only the two schools with mixed ethnic populations were included in these analyses.

Incidence rates (using nominations-based enemies scores) showed that 32 percent of children with enemies had only same-ethnicity enmities, 17 percent had only cross-ethnicity enmities, and 3 percent had both types. Chi-square analyses showed that same-ethnicity enemy relationships were significantly more common than either cross-ethnicity relationships $[\chi^2(1) = 11.98, p < .0005]$ or having both types $[\chi^2(1) = 64.18, p < .0001]$. In addition, cross-ethnicity enemies were more common than having both types $[\chi^2(1) = 26.84, p < .0001]$. For ratings-based enemies relationships, 18 percent had only same ethnicity, 10 percent had cross-ethnicity, and 9 percent had both types. As with nominations-based enemies, chi-square analyses showed that same-ethnicity enemy relationships were significantly more common than either cross-ethnicity relationships $[\chi^2(1) = 6.06, p < .01]$ or having both types $[\chi^2(1) = 6.78, p < .01]$.

Nominations-Based Enemy Relationships. Same-ethnicity enemies were positively correlated with social impact, withdrawal, and immaturity and negatively correlated with social preference, likability, and helpfulness (rs ranging from $\pm.17$ to .34). Cross-race enemies were positively correlated with social impact, withdrawal, and aggression (rs ranging from $\pm.15$ to .28). When the two types of enemies relationships were entered into a multiple regression along with dislike nominations, same-ethnicity enemies provided no significant independent variance for any adjustment variable, while cross-race enemies significantly predicted only aggression ($sr = .15$). When predicting adjustment a year later, same-ethnicity enemies scores showed no significant correlations; cross-ethnicity enemies correlated negatively with aggression ($sr = -.17$). In multiple regressions, cross-race enemies significantly predicted decreases in aggression ($sr = -.20$) and in overactivity ($sr = -.17$). Semipartial correlations for same-ethnicity enemies were all close to zero, and all were nonsignificant.

Ratings-Based Enemy Relationships. Same-ethnicity enemies were positively correlated with concurrent immaturity and negatively correlated with social preference and likability (rs ranging from $\pm.14$ to .29). Cross-race enemies were positively correlated with social impact, anxiety, withdrawal, immaturity, and sadness and negatively correlated with social preference and likability (rs ranging from $\pm.15$ to .40). When the two types of enemy relationships were included in a multiple regression along with dislike nominations, same-ethnicity enemies provided significant independent prediction for likability ($sr = -.21$), and cross-ethnicity enemies did so for likability ($sr = -.21$), anxiety ($sr = .13$), aggression ($sr = -.20$), and sadness ($sr = .14$).

In predicting year 2 adjustment, neither type of enemies relationship was a significant independent predictor.

Summary. Contrary to expectations, cross-ethnicity enemies appeared to be associated with more problematic adjustment than same-ethnicity enemies. Internalizing problems (anxious and sad) were independently predicted by cross-ethnicity enemies (ratings based); this is the only set of analyses conducted in this study that was associated with these problems, beyond the effects of unidirectional dislike. When combined with the negative association with aggression (ratings based), these findings perhaps depict a submissive, victimization-prone profile for children with cross-ethnicity enemies. This speculative notion is offset by the nominations-based positive association between cross-ethnicity enemies and aggression; however, in year 2, nominations-based enemies were independently associated with decreases in aggression.

Adjustment from Other Perspectives. The analyses reported so far rely solely on peers as the source of information about adjustment. Although in measurement terms, the use of peer-rated predictors and criterion variables would be expected, if anything, to increase any obtained associations, it is possible that reports from other sources might provide a different view on adjustment and also on its association with mutual dislike.

Self-reports and teacher reports were obtained for a subset of the full sample at year 1; all neglected, rejected, controversial, and popular children were included, as well as a subset of average and unclassified children ($n = 160$). Measures administered were the Children's Depression Inventory (CDI; Kovacs, 1985), a self-report measure of depression, and the teacher-rated Revised Behavior Problem Checklist (RBPC; Quay and Peterson, 1987). The RBPC yields scores on the following subscales: conduct disorder, socialized aggression, attention problems, anxious withdrawal, motor excess, and psychotic behavior. Data analysis strategies were the same as for previous sections.

Nominations-Based Enemy Relationships. Enemies scores were positively correlated with teacher-reported conduct disorder, socialized aggression, attention problems, and motor excess (*r*s ranging from .16 to .28). In multiple regressions, enemies scores did not provide significant independent prediction beyond that contributed by dislike nominations for any variable; however, the combined variance of enemies scores with dislike nominations did reach significance when predicting concurrent socialized aggression [$R^2 = .08$, $F(2,162) = 6.98$, $p < .001$].

Ratings-Based Enemy Relationships. Significant correlations were obtained between enemies scores and self-reported depression on the CDI and teacher-reported anxious withdrawal (both, $r = .18$). Enemies scores did not provide significant independent prediction beyond that of dislike nominations in multiple regressions predicting adjustment, but the block of enemies scores together with dislike nominations was significant for anxious withdrawal [$R^2 = .05$, $F(2,155) = 3.91$, $p < .05$].

Summary. Neither nominations-based nor ratings-based enemies showed independent associations with teacher-rated or self-reported adjustment.

Enemies Moderated by Level of Dislike. It may be that having enemies is not sufficient to affect (or reflect) adjustment. Perhaps a child's degree of peer group acceptance has implications for the role that having enemies plays in adjustment; certainly, having enemies does not appear to be restricted to children with significant problems with peer relationships, suggesting that it may be possible for some children to have mutual antipathies without negative effects on their adjustment. To examine this hypothesis, dislike nominations were used to moderate enemies in predicting concurrent and longitudinal adjustment. Significant interactions (controlling for main effects) were interpreted using procedures recommended by Aiken and West (1991).

Table 6.4 shows significant Enemies by Dislike interactions, by gender and method of deriving enemies variables. Significant interactions were obtained more frequently for girls than for boys. With nominations-based enemies, girls showed a pattern where having enemies had no relation with adjustment (aggression in year 1 and sad in year 2) at high levels of dislike, but a negative relation with these adjustment problems at low levels of dislike (in essence, having enemies was a protective factor). This kind of buffering effect was also seen with ratings-based enemies, where, at low levels of dislike, having enemies (ratings based) was associated with lower levels of concurrent sadness. The converse was also true: at high levels of dislike, having enemies corresponded to higher levels of concurrent sadness. Similarly, having enemies (ratings based) was associated with increasing social preference for girls with low levels of dislike, while girls who were greatly disliked and had enemies showed decreasing social preference the following year. Finally, enemies were most associated with increasing social impact for girls who were very disliked, whereas girls who were low on dislike showed little correspondence between having enemies and their future social impact.

For boys, the year 1 interaction indicated that as they became more disliked, having enemies (ratings based) had a reduced association with their likability; conversely, for boys who were not disliked, having enemies had a greater association with how well liked they were within the peer group. A second interaction showed that as boys became less disliked, having enemies (ratings based) predicted increases in withdrawal in the coming year, whereas highly disliked boys with enemies would be expected to decrease their later withdrawal.

Summary and Implications

In this sample, having at least one mutual antipathy (enemy) relationship was quite common, particularly when children used likability ratings, a method affording unlimited choices. It was more common to have enemies

**Table 6.4. Relation of Enemies to Adjustment as a Function
of Level of Dislike**

Criterion Variables	F[a]	Low	Medium	High
		Level of Dislike[b]		
Girls (nominations)				
Aggression (year 1)	7.36*	−.31	−.13	.04
Sad (year 2)	4.59*	−.28	−.11	.07
Girls (ratings)				
Sad (year 1)	10.38**	−.17	.05	.27
Social Preference (year 2)	12.11**	.25	−.03	−.31
Social Impact (Year 2)	4.08*	−.03	.17	.36
Boys (ratings)				
Likeability (year 1)	4.24*	−.51	−.41	−.32
Withdrawal (year 2)	5.20*	.16	.04	−.08

Note: $*p < .05$. $**p < .01$. $***p < .005$.

[a]Asterisks in this column indicate a significant interaction (Enemies by Dislike) controlling for main effects. For year 2 criterion variables, year 1 levels of adjustment were controlled.

[b]Procedures outlined by Aiken and West (1991) were used to interpret continuous interactions. Results are reported as standardized beta weights representing the relationship between number of enemies and adjustment at various levels of rejection (that is, negative nominations).

relationships for older elementary children than for younger; it is unclear whether this represents a developmental trend or is idiosyncratic to this sample. Perhaps most unexpectedly, it was apparent that being well accepted by the peer group at large (that is, being classified as sociometrically popular or average) did not preclude the existence of enemy relationships. This finding supported previous findings (Hembree and Vandell, 2000).

The primary goal of this study was to examine the hypothesis that children having enemy relationships would incur additional developmental risk, beyond the well-established risk for adjustment problems involved with being the subject of unilateral dislike. Although enemies relationships frequently were associated with adjustment variables, these correlations often proved to be due to the shared variance with dislike nominations; enemies demonstrated independent predictive utility in only a few instances. Most often, enemies were independently related to concurrent measures of peer acceptance (and not just to the particular variables used to create the enemies scores). In general, having enemies was associated with additional lack of acceptance within the peer group. Despite this, having enemies did not relate to prosocial behavior, not even in a negative direction, as also reported by Parker and Gamm (Chapter Four, this volume). Given that even well-accepted children had enemies, it is reasonable that lack of social skills would not be a necessary condition for having such relationships. Surprisingly, having enemies seemed to be linked with lowered social impact. Although it might be reasoned that being engaged in enmities might raise a child's social profile, in fact, having enemies was often related to being withdrawn. This supports the suggestion that a common strategy for managing an enemy relationship is to avoid the enemy (Chapter One, this volume).

Although aggression has previously been identified as being characteristic of children with enemies (Abecassis and others, 2002), findings were mixed in this sample. Using nominations-based enemies scores, there was a positive association with aggression for boys (total number of enemies, as well as mixed-sex enemies). However, using ratings-based enemies scores, concurrent links with aggression were consistently in a negative direction (full sample, girls, mixed-sex enemies for girls, mixed ethnicity school, and cross-ethnicity enemies). It is interesting to speculate about the process that might underlie the latter finding; possibly children can sometimes circumvent aggressive exchanges by understanding that particular classmates are enemies and by behaving accordingly, including avoiding them. Yet another perspective is offered by Parker and Gamm (Chapter Four, this volume), who found no significant association between enemies and aggression once the effects of rejection were controlled. Clearly more work is needed to explicate the processes involved with aggressive interactions between enemies.

Although it was expected that having enemies would be inherently stressful to children, resulting in internalizing outcomes such as depression, sadness, and anxiety, this hypothesis was largely unsupported here. This was true regardless of the source of information: peer report, teacher report, or self-report.

In addition, there were few longitudinal effects of having enemies beyond the impact of group-level dislike. The most consistent finding was a prediction of withdrawal, but the direction of the effect was mixed: same-sex enemies for boys and mixed-sex enemies for girls were associated with decreases in withdrawal, while total number of enemies for girls and for children in the Anglo school predicted increases in withdrawal during the following school year.

It is difficult to interpret this scattering of findings, particularly when some of them are contrary to expectations. Overall, there does not appear to be strong support for a robust association between having enemies and children's adjustment across a range of social, emotional, and behavioral outcomes (at least, after general dislike is accounted for). But perhaps this suggests that the wrong question has been asked. Instead, it may be more useful to identify circumstances, or types of children, for whom enemy relationships are harmful (Hartup and Abecassis, 2002). Some of the findings reported here are suggestive that this would be a profitable approach. For example, it was interesting to note that Hispanic children had the lowest incidence of enemies relationships. Furthermore, there were few independent associations between enemies scores and adjustment for this group (and, in fact, nominations-based enemies did not even significantly correlate with adjustment, even before the effects of dislike nominations were removed).

Even more intriguing were findings indicating that having enemies may be protective for some children at some times. The interactions between enemies and dislike expanded on the general finding that enemies were sometimes associated with lowered aggression. This seemed to be true especially for girls who were not disliked. Similarly, girls who were not disliked but had enemies were less likely to be sad, either at the time or the following year. Moreover, girls low on dislike who had enemies were likely to increase in peer group liking the following year. Perhaps there is a degree of assertiveness that is involved with identifying one's enemies and taking appropriate steps to manage such difficult relationships so that they do not interfere with daily life. If having enemies is as common as it appears to be, even among children who are well situated within the social group, then there must be prosocial ways of handling this situation. If so, this would explain why there does not seem to be a simple relationship between having enemies and experiencing adjustment problems.

This study contrasted two methods for identifying enemies relationships. Enemies scores based on mutual dislike nominations did not demonstrate much independent prediction beyond the effects of unilateral dislike; counting just the multiple regression analyses, only 5 percent of these resulted in significant findings for enemies scores. Obviously, it is difficult to make a case for the validity of this set of findings. The enemies scores based on mutual low likability ratings were more successful, showing significant independent prediction in 16 percent of the regressions. The reason might simply be that there was less shared variance between dislike nominations and enemies scores not based on dislike nominations. Beyond this, researchers need to consider what would constitute a more valid measure of mutual antipathy. The case could be made that nominations would result in the naming of the most saliently disliked classmates, because children are asked to use recall to generate the names. On the other hand, some have argued that requiring children to make a rating of each classmate results in a more valid assessment of liking because no one is inadvertently left out of the rating process. Certainly, the ratings method resulted in higher incidence rates of enemy relationships, and the greater range in scores could in itself account for the increased number of significant findings. The methodological issues in measuring enemy relationships are far from resolved.

A related issue is the conceptual basis for identifying children's enemy relationships. It is, of course, a leap to use the term *enemy* for the mutual dislike pairings described in this study. Careful conceptualization of the enemy construct must be done. Must an enemy relationship be characterized by other negative feelings, such as anger? How intensely must one dislike an enemy? Would a simple and clear preference not to interact with another person, but without feelings of hatred or distress, constitute an enemy relationship if the other person felt the same way?

Just as researchers need to be clearer about their own ideas about enemies, we also need to find out more about children's ideas about enemies.

We know virtually nothing about children's conceptions of enemies. Do children themselves consider mutual antipathies to constitute an enemy relationship? How often are children fully aware that those they dislike return the sentiment? Similarly, we know little about the circumstances surrounding enemy relationships. Does it bother children when someone they dislike also dislikes them? To what extent do children avoid or engage their enemies? How much conflict is typical between enemies? Is conflict within an enemy relationship more (or less) distressing and harmful than conflict within other kinds of relationships?

The results reported here clearly suggest that looking for simple relationships between a child's having one or more enemies and that child's social and behavioral adjustment is not likely to lead to better conceptions of adjustment or of inimical relationships. In order to understand links between having enemies and adjustment better, we need to examine contextual issues (Chapter Three, this volume) as well as the nature of interactions between enemies (Chapters Two and Four, this volume) and the process of such relationships over time (Chapter Five, this volume). Only by identifying the mechanisms involved whereby some children suffer from being involved in enemy relationships (and others perhaps benefit from the same kinds of relationships) will we be able to advance our understanding of mutual dislike as a factor in children's adjustment.

References

Abecassis, M., and others. "Mutual Antipathies and Their Developmental Significance in Middle Childhood and Adolescence." *Child Development*, 2002, 73, 1543–1556.

Aiken, L. S., and West, S. G. *Multiple Regression: Testing and Interpreting Interactions.* Thousand Oaks, Calif.: Sage, 1991.

Asher, S. R., and Hymel, S. "Children's Social Competence in Peer Relations: Sociometric and Behavioral Assessment." In J. D. Wine and M. D. Smye (eds.), *Social Competence.* New York: Guilford Press, 1981.

Bierman, K. L., and Welsh, J. A. "Social Relationship Deficits." In E. J. Mash and L. G. Terdal (eds.), *Assessment of Childhood Disorders.* New York: Guilford Press, 1997.

Bukowski, W. M., Pizzamiglio, M. T., Newcomb, A. F., and Hoza, B. "Popularity as an Affordance for Friendship: The Link Between Group and Dyadic Experience." *Social Development*, 1996, 5, 191–204.

Bukowski, W. M., Sippola, L., Hoza, B., and Newcomb, A. F. "Pages from a Sociometric Notebook: An Analysis of Nomination and Rating Scale Measures of Acceptance, Rejection, and Social Preferences." In A.H.N. Cillessen and W. M. Bukowski (eds.), *Recent Advancements in the Measurement of Acceptance and Rejection in the Peer System.* New Directions for Child and Adolescent Development, no. 88. San Francisco: Jossey-Bass, 2000.

Coie, J. D., Dodge, K. A., and Coppotelli, H. "Dimensions and Types of Social Status: A Cross-Age Perspective." *Developmental Psychology*, 1982, 18, 557–570.

Eder, D., and Hallinan, M. T. "Sex Differences in Children's Friendships." *American Sociological Review*, 1978, 43, 237–250.

Falicov, C. J. "Ethnicity and Family Therapy." In M. McGoldrick, J. K. Pearce, and J. Giordano (eds.), *Mexican Families.* New York: Guilford Press, 1982.

Hartup, W. W. "The Peer System." In E. M. Hetherington (vol. ed.), *Handbook of Child*

Psychology, Vol. 4. Socialization, Personality and Social Development. (4th ed.) New York: Wiley, 1983.

Hartup, W. W., and Abecassis, M. "Friends and Enemies." In P. K. Smith and C. H. Hart (eds.), *Blackwell Handbook of Childhood Social Development.* Cambridge, Mass.: Blackwell, 2002.

Hembree, S. E., and Vandell, D. L. "Reciprocity in Rejection: The Role of Mutual Antipathy and Children's Adjustment." Unpublished manuscript, University of Wisconsin, 2000.

Kovacs, M. "The Children's Depression Inventory." *Psychopharmacology Bulletin,* 1985, *21,* 995–998.

Maccoby, E. E., and Jacklin, C. N. "Gender Segregation in Childhood." In H. Reese (ed.), *Advances in Child Development and Behavior.* Orlando, Fla.: Academic Press, 1987.

Pope, A. W., and Bierman, K. L. "Predicting Adolescent Peer Problems and Antisocial Activities: The Relative Roles of Aggression and Dysregulation." *Developmental Psychology,* 1999, *35,* 335–346.

Powlishta, K. K., Serbin, L. A., Doyle, A., and White, D. C. "Gender, Ethnic, and Body Type Biases: The Generality of Prejudice in Children." *Developmental Psychology,* 1994, *30,* 526–536.

Quay, H., and Peterson, D. *Manual for the Revised Behavior Problem Checklist.* Coral Gables, Fla., 1987.

Rotenberg, K. J. "Same-Sex Patterns and Sex Differences in the Trust-Value Basis of Children's Friendship." *Sex Roles,* 1986, *15,* 613–626.

Rubin, K. H., Bukowski, W., and Parker, J. G. "Peer Interactions, Relationships, and Groups." In W. Damon (series ed.) and N. Eisenberg (ed.), *Handbook of Child Psychology: Vol. 3. Social, Emotional, and Personality Development.* New York: Wiley, 1998.

ALICE W. POPE is an associate professor of psychology at St. John's University, Jamaica, New York.

7

Relationships based on aversion and antipathy may turn out to have major developmental implications, but more refined analysis is needed to support this assertion.

Toward Understanding Mutual Antipathies in Childhood and Adolescence

Willard W. Hartup

Close relationships among children and adolescents are ordinarily considered to encompass friendliness and fun. Recent studies, however, reveal that many friendships have dark sides consisting of competitiveness, hostility, and conflict. These attributes attenuate the contributions made by friendship experience to good developmental outcome (Berndt, Hawkins, and Jiao, 1999) and increase aggression and antisocial behavior (Dishion, Andrews, and Crosby, 1995).

Social networks among children and adolescents also include relationships that are not based on social attraction at all, but rather are rooted in antipathy, animosity, and enmity. The term *mutual antipathies* describes this general category of relationships in which children and certain associates identify one another as persons whom they do not like. These mutual antipathies form a superordinate class of social relationships that encompasses "being enemies," as well as other relationships maintained on the basis of social aversion.

Early studies of mutual antipathies and their developmental significance, including those described in this book, have raised a number of questions. We examine seven in this chapter:

1. Conceptualization and methodology. Although some attention has been given to the need for making distinctions between relationship categories such as mutual antipathies, enemies, animosities, and aversions, considerable conceptual and methodological confusion still exists among

methods for identifying mutual antipathies and the involvement of individuals in them.

2. Salience. Although the existence of mutual antipathies is believed to be relatively common during childhood and adolescence, their salience in the lives of children needs to be more clearly established.

3. Heterogeneity. Heterogeneities among mutual antipathies need to be identified in terms of several different dimensions or features of these relationships, for example, what enemies do and do not do together, similarities and differences between them, and the nature of their affective involvement with one another.

4. Dynamics. The social dynamics that characterize various types of mutual antipathies are completely undocumented. We need to know something about the social exchange processes and interpersonal understanding occurring between individuals who are involved with one another in mutual antipathies or as enemies.

5. Antecedents. Conditions predisposing children and adolescents to involvement in mutual antipathies need to be identified, including personality characteristics and relationship antecedents (for example, parent-child relationships, friendships, earlier enmities).

6. Correlates. Does involvement in mutual antipathies account for individual variation in social adaptation that is not already accounted for by peer acceptance and rejection generally?

7. Developmental course. When, in developmental terms, do these relationships matter, and why? Developmental models are needed in order to specify the manner in which involvement in mutual antipathies combines over time with temperament and early experience, family relationships, friendships and peer experience, the social context, and emerging social competence in child and adolescent development.

Given the short time that mutual antipathies have received research attention, more of these questions are unanswerable than are.

Conceptual and Methodological Issues

The English language provides a number of constructs with which to refer to "negative" or "aversive" relationships. Abecassis (Chapter One, this volume) writes about the difference between mutual antipathies, on the one hand, and enmities, on the other. Dictionaries, she points out, tell us that antipathies involve less hostility and animosity than enmities, as well as less threat and implied aggressiveness. Both relationship categories involve mutual dislike, but one (antipathies) is superordinate to the other (enemies).

Even a quick survey of research on these negative relationships reveals a chaotic situation with respect to the terms used in relation to the methods employed. One group of investigators uses *mutual antipathies* to refer to relationships identified by asking children or adolescents to nominate others whom they "do not like at all" (Abecassis and others, 2002). Others use *mutual antipathies* to describe dyads identified by asking respondents to nominate others who are "liked least" (Schwartz, Hopmeyer-Gorman, Toblin, and Abou-ezzeddine, Chapter Three, this volume). Still other investigators use *mutual antipathies* to refer to relationships identified by nominations of children the respondent does not want to play with (Hembree and Vandell, 2000).

In contrast, the word *enemies* is preferred by other investigators even when dyads are identified in ways that are the same as those described above. *Enemies* is the word used by Hayes, Gershman, and Bolin (1980) to describe children who mention one another on a sociometric interview as "someone you don't like." Other investigators have used *enemies* to refer to dyads identified by mutual nominations of individuals as liked least in their classes (Pope, Chapter Six, this volume); *animosities,* however, is the term preferred by other investigators (Rodkin, Pearl, Farmer, and Van Acker, Chapter Five, this volume) for dyads identified in this same way. Still other investigators (Card and Hodges, Chapter Two, this volume) identify enemies in terms of mutual nominations of individuals whom the respondent does not want to play with. Finally, some investigators use the terms *mutual antipathies* and *enemies* interchangeably to refer to relationships identified by classmate ratings on scales varying between "like very much" and "don't like at all" (Parker and Gamm, Chapter Four, this volume).

In other words, there is no correlation between the relationship constructs used in this literature and the methods used to identify the relevant dyads. Moreover, some of the least conservative methods for identifying aversive relationships (nominating children who are "liked least" or children "you don't want to play with") are used by certain investigators to identify relationships that are considered to be weighted with the most hostility and negative affect (that is, enemies, animosities).

One can make the case that no one thus far has actually studied enemies. Abecassis (Chapter One, this volume) argues that while the mutual antipathies construct subsumes the enemies or animosities construct, the reverse is not true. Accordingly, everyone in this research area (including everyone represented in this volume) has studied mutual antipathies regardless of how the relationship is labeled in the researcher's manuscript. Whether this inconsistency should be deplored is an empirical question— but an empirical question that is surprisingly difficult to answer. Studies in which dyads composed of individuals who dislike one another but do not regard themselves as enemies are necessary to use these terms interchangeably as investigators are now doing.

Asking youngsters to identify one another as enemies, however, may be unethical. Most investigators assume that doing this would be potentially harmful to some children and their relationships. Abecassis (Chapter One, this volume) suggests several ways for asking questions beyond "Who do you not like?" that may assist in locating actual enemies: asking about the nature of the interaction and affect occurring between the child and various partners. Steps in this direction are crucial not only to obtain a more consistent terminology in this research area, but to determine how social reality is cognitively mapped. At this time, we do not know whether children and adolescents consistently perceive and interact with associates whom they dislike in different ways from people they hate or regard as enemies. The fact that the English language differentiates among these types of relationships does not mean that social reality is psychologically parsed in the same way.

Methodological inconsistency poses as much difficulty in furthering this research field as conceptual looseness. Sociometric testing now favors nominations of classmates whom respondents "like least" as a method of measuring peer rejection. Some of us have used such nominations, when two children use them mutually, to identify children who dislike each other without realizing that these nominations may single out some children who simply do not share interests or common ground of any kind, or children who both have little social impact. In other words, one can question the use of "liked-least" nominations to identify mutual antipathies because in some cases, these methods will yield false positives (that is, mutual antipathies in which no disliking is involved). Similarly, naming one another as nonpreferred play partners or nonpreferred partners for school trips or projects does not always identify a mutual antipathy, let alone enemies. These methods certainly identify some dyads in which the children do not like one another, but undoubtedly also dyads in which the children are indifferent to one another or merely unlike one another. Considerable methodological confusion, then, stands in the way of understanding mutual antipathies. Given the newness of this research area, methodological diversity may need to be encouraged. The beginnings, however, seem haphazard.

Salience

Children and adolescents spend more time with their friends than with other associates (Hinde, Titmus, Easton, and Tamplin, 1985), and these relationships are known to classmates and sometimes to teachers and parents. Mutual antipathies are frequently veiled in avoidance and are sometimes visible only in the form of bully-victim interaction or persistent fighting. Such variations make it extremely difficult to infer the existence of mutual antipathies, let alone their importance to the children or adolescents involved.

Research progress to date has depended exclusively on the sociometric ratings or nominations described previously. When mutual antipathies (or enemies) were identified by the investigators contributing to this book, no other information was obtained to confirm that the children involved actually recognized these relationships as reciprocated rejection or, indeed, whether they recognized them as relationships at all. Even when the results suggest that children and their enemies are different from one another in their "relationship orientations" (Card and Hodges, Chapter Two, this volume), we do not know whether the children were aware of these differences between them. Once again, answers to a simple question ("Are mutual antipathies identified by sociometric methods salient to the children involved?") are difficult to obtain. Children can certainly be asked about how they characterize designated classmates and what their interactions with them are like. Observations can also be used to determine interaction styles among children who do not like each other, including the frequency with which they exhibit negative social exchanges, hostility, fighting, disparagement, and so forth. One of the greatest needs at this moment, then, is to establish the salient social dynamics that underlie these relationships.

Sheer incidence tells us whether mutual antipathies constitute a substantial segment of children's social networks. Summarizing the current results is not easy owing to method differences, but an attempt to do so is contained in the following paragraphs. First, almost nothing is known about the incidence of mutual antipathies among preschool-aged children. Hayes, Gershman, and Bolin (1980) used interviews to study young children's dislike of their associates, but mutual disliking was an extremely rare occurrence. Fighting within particular dyads of this age is also rare (Ross and Conant, 1992). Sociometric interviews and observed fighting, though, both have their drawbacks as bases for inferring the existence of mutual enmities among young children (Hymel, 1983; Ross and Conant, 1992). Until some better techniques are invented for identifying these relationships among preschool children, we must conclude that the evidence is too thin to draw conclusions.

Second, among school-aged children, prevalence rates reported by the various investigators are variable and impossible to compare owing to differences in methodology. Six investigators and their colleagues have examined incidence using nominations procedures. Rates for children ranging from ages eight through eleven vary from 15 percent (Rodkin, Pearl, Farmer, and Van Acker, Chapter Five, this volume, for eight year olds) to 65 percent (Hembree and Vandell, 2000) with a median of 30 percent (Abecassis and others, 2002; Pope, Chapter Six, this volume; and Rodkin, Pearl, Farmer, and Van Acker, Chapter Five, this volume, for nine year olds). Rates are similar for fourteen year olds when nominations procedures are used (Abecassis and others, 2002).

Third, substantially higher rates (58 percent and 67 percent) were obtained when ratings rather than nominations are used to identify mutual antipathies (Parker and Gamm, Chapter Four, this volume; Pope, Chapter Six, this volume). These higher rates undoubtedly reflect the lack of an arbitrary cut-off in number of individuals evaluated that is inherent in the use of sociometric ratings as compared with sociometric nominations.

Fourth, incidence rates vary according to gender and age. Gender moderates the incidence of mutual antipathies in two ways: sex of the individual children being studied and gender composition of the antipathetic dyads themselves (same or mixed sex). According to Rodkin, Pearl, Farmer, and Van Acker (Chapter Five, this volume), about 50 percent of third-grade children's antipathies are same sex, with this number rising by 8 percent when the children reach fourth grade, mostly due to an increase in same-sex antipathies among boys. Abecassis and others (2002) found that fifth-grade boys were more frequently involved in same-sex antipathies (25 percent) than girls (9 percent), a difference that was narrower among eighth graders. No significant gender or age differences were obtained, however, for involvement in mixed-sex antipathies. Skimpy as these results are, one can nevertheless argue that the existence of mutual antipathies and enmities must be studied with attention to variations between the sexes as well as developmentally.

Overall, we know that the incidence of mutual antipathies among children and adolescents in classrooms is greater than can be expected by chance (Abecassis and others, 2002). While there is some difference in incidence rates reported, one can guess that overall estimates of approximately 30 percent are likely to hold through future studies, although incidence rates for various groups (age, sex, ethnicity, school and class size, socioeconomic status) are likely to make general rates a poor method to use in describing the salience of these relationships. Whether the incidence of mutual antipathies among children and adolescents should be regarded as "large" or "small," "to-be-expected" or "worrisome," is too early to say. One should note that the obtained mutual antipathy rates exceed the number of children who are found to be socially rejected in sociometric studies (about 15 percent) and are at risk in the development of aggression and antisocial behavior. Although it would help to know more about the salience of mutual antipathies among children and adolescents themselves, their incidence suggests that these relationships should not be ignored.

Heterogeneity

Mutual antipathies come in many flavors. Although investigators like to generalize about them, the nature of these relationships varies a great deal. Both their histories and the interactions characterizing them are diverse. Some enmities are marked by bullying and victimization; some not. Some enmities are marked by squabbling and fighting; others not. Some are marked by avoidance; others not.

One framework that may be useful in thinking about these heterogeneities consists of "levels of complexity" (Hinde, 1979). Among the dimensions of relationships that this framework encompasses are content, diversity, patterning, affective quality, similarity, intimacy, commitment, and interpersonal perception. These are all dimensions along which relationships can differ from one another and which may determine their longevity and their significance in development and adaptation:

• Content. At the moment, the content of mutual antipathies has not been documented or the conditions specified that are responsible for variations in it. It matters greatly, however, whether these relationships involve fighting and harassment, victimization, or avoidance. Content specifics are high on the agenda of research needed on these relationships.

• Diversity. Diversity, which means the number of different kinds of interaction that characterize a relationship, should also be studied since some enmities seem to be marked by differences in interests and attitudes between the participants, while others also involve avoidance and, sometimes, aggression. Enmities that are marked only by dissimilarities are likely to be very different from those that also include agonistic attitudes and behavior.

• Quality. Affective quality also varies from mutual antipathy to mutual antipathy. Abecassis (Chapter One, this volume) discusses the likelihood that some enmities contain very little affect beyond mild aversion, while others are marked by deep hatred. Some enmities may carry anxiety, uncertainty, and fear; others indifference. Given that these affective heterogeneities may differentiate those relationships that constitute risk factors from those that do not, investigators need to find ways to conceptualize and measure them.

• Patterns. This term refers to the totality of constituent interactions between two enemies and may be relevant to their social adaptation. Mutual antipathies are different, for example, when they involve social contact, demands, and hostility as compared to avoidance and bad-mouthing. Children use covariations (patterns) such as these to construct attributional hypotheses; thus, patterns occurring in the interactions between two individuals carry implications for the manner in which their relationship will be perceived and labeled. The psychological consequences of certain clusters of interactions may also differ from other clusters. For example, the amount of aggression directed from one enemy to another may not be as important as the contingencies in the interaction between them (Hartup and Sancilio, 1986). Needless to say, no one has studied the many ways in which mutual antipathies are patterned.

• Similarity between enemies. One question about mutual antipathies that begs for an answer is the extent to which they involve children who are different or similar to one another. Card and Hodges (Chapter Two, this volume) present intriguing evidence that the relationship orientation of children with their respective parents differs more within inimical dyads than within other ones. They argue that relationship orientations are salient in children's interpersonal relations and that when two children find themselves to be different or incompatible in their relationship expectations (with parents especially), aversion and enmity are likely. These authors suggest that enemies may be different from one another in other ways, although evidence dealing with this issue is scarce.

In one ongoing investigation (Van Lieshout and others, 2003), mutual antipathies among adolescents were characterized by greater differences between the individuals involved than between "neutral classmates" or between friends. Greater differences were obtained in antisocial behavior and social withdrawal as well as prosocial behavior and achievement. Such results are not unexpected since it is already known that children are more likely to dislike others who are perceived as being different from themselves than those who are perceived as similar (Rosenbaum, 1986). As Card and Hodges (Chapter Two, this volume) point out, however, the association between dissimilarity and enmity is moderate; enemy dyads vary greatly from one another in the extent to which individuals involved are different. The developmental significance of these variations, however, is unknown.

• Intimacy and commitment. Intimacy and commitment are relationship dimensions of considerable significance in friendships and romantic relationships. In contrast, these constructs scarcely apply to mutual antipathies. One can imagine instances in which children who dislike one another also share confidences or deliberately seek to maintain their inimical relationship. Speculation about these situations nevertheless seems premature.

• Interpersonal perception. Mutual antipathies involve interpersonal perceptions that undoubtedly differ greatly from one relationship to another. In general, enemies are regarded as power assertive, threatening, and uncooperative. When asked how they would make requests of enemies or friends, respectively, school-aged children said they would be less direct and imperative in persuading enemies. Seemingly, children think that one should approach enemies with caution, similar to the caution used with other persons who have greater power and authority than they do (Cowan, Drinkard, and MacGavin, 1984). Children also attribute motives to their enemies that are more hostile than motives attributed to friends or acquaintances. For example, when one gets hurt in an ambiguous situation, the intentions of enemies are believed to be more hostile than those of friends or acquaintances; victims are expected to retaliate more frequently (Ray and Cohen, 1997). Such attribution biases suggest that children assume the worst of their enemies. Dyadic differences in these attributions have never been studied.

Dynamics

Little is known about the social interaction that occurs between children involved in mutual antipathies, assuming they interact at all. Social exchange processes, contagion, modeling, and communication between enemies have not been examined either normatively or across different kinds of animosities (for example, bully-victim relationships, broken friendships, ex-romances, attitude dissimilarities). This void could be partially filled if investigators would conduct several kinds of studies: (1)

playground observations of children who mutually nominate one another as disliked or who in some other ways indicate that they dislike one another; (2) laboratory observations of social interaction during joint problem solving between children who do not like one another, including the talk that passes between them and the kinds of persuasion and influence attempts that are made; and (3) "enemy interviews," in which children are asked to describe their interactions with others who are mutually disliked. These methods have yielded invaluable information concerning the social dynamics involved in children's friendships (see Marshall and McCandless, 1957; Berndt, 1986; Dishion, Andrews, and Crosby, 1995) and can readily be adapted to mutual antipathies.

Antecedents

Antecedents of mutual antipathies can be divided into two classes: distal and proximal. Distal antecedents include predisposing conditions such as the social competence and personality characteristics of the child, the social conditions in which children live, relationship histories within the family, and the nature of earlier experiences with other children. Since longitudinal data are required to identify these distal conditions, we know virtually nothing about these antecedents of mutual antipathies involvement. Earlier aggression seems to be a risk factor for developing these antipathies, although the relevant longitudinal evidence spans only a short time (Rodkin, Pearl, Farmer, and Van Acker, Chapter Five, this volume). Attachment relations with parents have been suggested as predisposing children toward having enemies (Card and Hodges, Chapter Two, this volume), but the only evidence consists of cross-sectional correlations between children's interviews concerning relationship stance and sociometrically derived measures of antipathies involvement.

Similarly intriguing are questions having to do with the inciting incidents that precipitate a mutual antipathy. How important are betrayals and broken promises as proximal antecedents of mutual antipathies? Bullying and victimization? Dissimilarities in interests and attitudes? What incidents mark the beginnings of mutual antipathies, strengthen them, or weaken them? These variations (see Abecassis, Chapter One, this volume) are important in understanding the genesis of these relationships and the social dynamics marking them. Developmental implications may also differ. Close tracking of children's social choices and their interactions with one another could tell us much about these questions.

Correlates

The relation between mutual antipathies and the social adjustment of the child is a central concern in this book. Some seven investigators have examined this issue using a variety of methods and strategies. The results are not uniform. No one has found that involvement in mutual antipathies is positively associated with the quality of social adaptation in childhood or adolescence, except in a small set of exploratory analyses (Pope, Chapter Six, this volume). To the contrary, investigators have found either negative relations between these variables or no significant relations at all.

Almost everyone has found that involvement in mutual antipathies is negatively associated with social acceptance or likability (Rodkin, Pearl, Farmer, and Van Acker, Chapter Five, this volume; Parker and Gamm, Chapter Four, this volume). (Popularity as rated by teachers, a different construct, is not related to involvement in mutual antipathies, however. Rodkin, Pearl, Farmer, and Van Acker, Chapter Five, this volume.)

The weight of the evidence also shows that involvement in mutual antipathies is positively correlated with peer rejection or being generally disliked (Hembree and Vandell, 2000; Abecassis and others, 2002; Rodkin, Pearl, Farmer, and Van Acker, Chapter Five, this volume; Pope, Chapter Six, this volume). Some confounding underlies these results, however. Since most investigators have identified mutual antipathies by means of children's nominations as "not liked" or "liked least" and since the child's sociometric status is based partially on these same nominations, it follows that involvement in a mutual antipathy should be more common among socially rejected children than among others. This confounding is not complete, though, so the importance of these results is not totally compromised.

Categorical measures of sociometric status taking both social acceptance and social rejection into account reveal that children with mutual antipathies are overrepresented in some categories and underrepresented in others. Overrepresentation occurs among controversial and rejected children and underrepresentation among popular, average, and neglected children (Hembree and Vandell, 2000; Abecassis and others, 2002; Pope, Chapter Six, this volume). One condition, however, needs to be recognized: while being generally disliked and unpopular (or controversial) are among the strongest correlates of involvement in mutual antipathies, substantial numbers of popular and average children are also involved in them. Estimates vary widely, ranging from 13 percent (Pope, Chapter Six, this volume) to 32 percent (Hembree and Vandell, 2000), as the proportion of popular children who are involved in these relationships. These discrepancies aside, though, having enemies is clearly not limited to children whose group-level peer relations are problematic.

Two large-scale studies of eight, eleven, and fourteen year olds (Hembree and Vandell, 2000; Abecassis and others, 2002) show that with peer rejection held constant, involvement in mutual antipathies is associated with antisocial behavior and social withdrawal among children and adolescents of both sexes and to emotionality and lack of friendship support among adolescents. School achievement is also negatively associated with antipathies involvement among the eight and fourteen year olds. Two more narrowly focused studies show a relation between involvement in mutual antipathies and aggression, but with important qualifications: (1) aggression is greater among children with mutual antipathies in environments that expose them frequently to aggression but not in more peaceful ones (Schwartz, Hopmeyer-Gorman, Toblin, and Abou-ezzddine, Chapter Three, this volume), and (2) when antipathies involvement increases over time, aggression also increases (Rodkin, Pearl, Farmer, and Van Acker, Chapter Five, this volume). In two other studies, aggression and prosocial behavior were found not to be correlated with antipathies involvement, at least when general peer rejection was factored out (Parker and Gamm, Chapter Four, this volume; Pope, Chapter Six, this volume).

Based on these studies, one can state provisionally that mutual antipathies are concomitants of risk in both childhood and adolescence, but results are not entirely consistent. Effect sizes, relative to the amount of variance in social adaptation attributable to peer rejection, are generally small. Differences in outcomes are not correlated with differences in methodology or strategy except that the most comprehensive studies have been those reporting significant associations between social adaptation and involvement in mutual antipathies. Clearly, the last word concerning the relation between antipathies and social adjustment is not in. Every reason exists, however, to continue to hypothesize that mutual antipathies have questionable value to those who are involved in them.

Developmental Course

Does involvement in mutual antipathies during childhood and adolescence make any difference to the individual in the long run? Are adolescents and adults who have been involved in many inimical relationships at greater risk for antisocial behavior, depression, relationship problems, and parenting difficulties than individuals involved to a lesser extent? Are there times in individual development when coping with enemies presents a greater challenge than at others? What are the synergies, in development, among parent-child relationships, peer relationships (including friendships), and relations with enemies?

None of these questions can be answered at the moment. Most writers (see Hartup and Abecassis, 2002) believe that the personalized and dyadic rejection that marks mutual antipathies constitutes a developmental challenge, especially when children have many mutual enemies. Developmental risk may also be greater among individuals who are disposed for other reasons to become antisocial or depressed adults. Quite possibly, too, children who have general difficulties in social development are also likely to generate mutual antipathies. In other words, causal direction in social development is likely to be two way in this instance rather than one way. Finally, the heterogeneities that mark human development in general (Hartup and Van Lieshout, 1995) make it probable that these relationships have greater developmental significance for some children than others. Although answers to these questions require considerable effort and ingenuity, they are achievable.

Conclusion

Studies conducted thus far suggest that mutual antipathies contribute to social development and are salient to children and adolescents themselves. Correlational evidence is difficult to use as a basis for strong causal inferences, and it is too soon to make the preceding assertion without some caution. Nevertheless, some of the most notorious children in recent memory (for example, school shooters) have been disliked, victimized, and involved in mutual antipathies. School violence, of course, is multidetermined behavior. But if we want to boost outcome prediction in this area, we can hypothesize even now that children's experiences with their enemies as well as with their friends should be included in contemporary developmental models.

Mutual antipathies need to be differentiated from one another in terms of their histories and the affects that pervade them. Conditions predisposing children and adolescents to mutual antipathies need to be specified and sex differences better described. Moderating effects of friendships on the importance of mutual antipathies need to be studied, as well as the reverse. Especially needed is some inkling of how friendship involvement interacts with antipathy involvement, given that a substantial number of popular and average children are involved in mutual antipathies. Finally, we need detailed information about the social exchange dynamics existing between children who do not like one another—both what they expect of one another and what actually happens.

Although enemies probably make different developmental contributions from friends, these two kinds of relationships probably complement one another rather than compete in determining the manner in which a child or adolescent acts within and across situations. Some friendships have dark sides themselves; hence, this task requires comprehensive and nuanced research strategies. Although it may be early to assert that enemies are as important to the development of social competence as friends are, it is not too early to guess that for some children, they are.

References

Abecassis, M., and others. "Mutual Antipathies and Their Developmental Significance in Middle Childhood and Adolescence." *Child Development*, 2002, 73, 1543–1556.

Berndt, T. J. "Children's Comments About Their Friends." In M. Perlmutter (ed.), *Cognitive Perspectives on Children's Social and Behavioral Development*. Mahwah, N.J.: Erlbaum, 1986.

Berndt, T. J., Hawkins, J. A., and Jiao, Z. "Influences of Friends and Friendship on Adjustment to Junior High School." *Merrill-Palmer Quarterly*, 1999, 45, 13–41.

Cowan, G., Drinkard, J., and MacGavin, L. "The Effect of Target, Age, and Gender on Use of Power Strategies." *Journal of Personality and Social Psychology,* 1984, *47,* 1391–1398.

Dishion, T. J., Andrews, D. W., and Crosby, L. "Anti-Social Boys and Their Friends in Early Adolescence: Relationship Characteristics, Quality, and Interactional Processes." *Child Development,* 1995, *66,* 139–151.

Hartup, W. W., and Abecassis, M. "Friends and Enemies." In P. K. Smith and C. H. Hart (eds.), *Blackwell's Handbook of Social Development.* Cambridge, Mass.: Blackwell, 2002.

Hartup, W. W., and Sancilio, M. F. "Children's Friendships." In E. Schopler and G. B. Mesibov (eds.), *Social Behavior in Autism.* New York: Plenum, 1986.

Hartup, W. W., and Van Lieshout, C.F.M. "Personality Development in Social Context." *Annual Review of Psychology,* 1995, *46,* 655–687.

Hayes, D., Gershman, E., and Bolin, L. "Friends and Enemies: Cognitive Bases for Preschool Children's Unilateral and Reciprocal Relationships." *Child Development,* 1980, *51,* 1276–1279.

Hembree, S. E., and Vandell, D. L. "Reciprocity in Rejection: The Role of Mutual Antipathy in Children's Adjustment." Unpublished manuscript, University of Wisconsin, 2000.

Hinde, R. A. *Towards Understanding Relationships.* Orlando, Fla.: Academic Press, 1979.

Hinde, R. A., Titmus, G., Easton, D., and Tamplin, A. "Incidence of 'Friendship' and Behavior with Strong Associates Versus Non-Associates in Preschoolers." *Child Development,* 1985, *56,* 234–245.

Hymel, S. "Preschool Children's Peer Relations: Issues in Sociometric Assessment." *Merrill-Palmer Quarterly,* 1983, *29,* 237–260.

Marshall, H. R., and McCandless, B. R. "A Study in Prediction of Social Behavior of Preschool Children." *Child Development,* 1957, *28,* 149–159.

Ray, G., and Cohen, R. "Children's Evaluations of Provocation Between Peers." *Aggressive Behavior,* 1997, *23,* 417–431.

Rosenbaum, M. E. "The Repulsion Hypothesis: On the Nondevelopment of Relationships." *Journal of Personality and Social Psychology,* 1986, *51,* 1156–1166.

Ross, H., and Conant, C. "The Social Structure of Early Conflicts: Interaction, Relationships, and Alliances." In C. U. Shantz and W. W. Hartup (eds.), *Conflict in Child and Adolescent Development.* Cambridge: Cambridge University Press, 1992.

Van Lieshout, C.F.M., and others. "Heterogeneity of Mutual Friendships and Mutual Antipathies: A Cross Sectional Study." Unpublished manuscript, 2003.

WILLARD W. HARTUP is professor emeritus in the Institute of Child Development, University of Minnesota, Minneapolis.

INDEX

Card, N. A., 2, 3, 23, 33, 78, 113, 115, 118
Carolina Longitudinal Study, 82
Cassidy, J., 25
CEQ. *See* Community Experience Questionnaire (CEQ)
Children's Depression Inventory (CDI), 43, 104
Christopoulos, C., 40, 50, 69
Cillessen, T., 59, 74
Clark, K. B., 74
Clark, M. P., 74
Cognitive processing bias, 14
Cognitive skills, 1
Cohen, R., 12, 15, 17, 18, 33, 118
Coie, J. D., 23–24, 40, 41, 50, 58, 65, 69, 75, 90
Cole, A. K., 25
Communication, and avoidance of enemies, 17
Community Experience Questionnaire (CEQ), 42
Compas, B. E., 50, 51
Conant, C., 115
Contreras, J. M., 25
Controversial children, 15
Cooley, C. H., 73–74
Coppotelli, H., 75, 90
Cowan, G., 118
Crick, N., 14, 15, 16, 58
Crosby, L., 111, 119
Culture, 100–104
Curtis, R., 16

De Wolff, M., 24, 26, 34
Deater-Deckard, K., 40
DeLawyer, D. D., 59, 70
Depression, 51
Developmental risk, 121–122
Disciplinary techniques, 23
Dishion, T. J., 111, 119
Disliking: and aggression, 107; commonness in middle childhood, 89; and development of self, 74; incidence of, 91–93; versus liking, 82; measures of, 90–91; reasons for, 82–83; and withdrawal, 105, 107
Disliking study: culture in, 100–104; ethnicity in, 100–104; gender in, 97–100; methods of, 90; results of, 90–96
Distal antecedents, 119
Dodge, K., 14, 15, 16, 23–24, 40, 41, 50, 58, 69, 74, 75, 90

Downey, G., 15
Doyle, A. B., 24, 98
Drinkard, J., 118
Duck, S., 8, 14, 15, 16, 17, 18, 19
Dyadic relationships: aggression in, 50; enmity's overlap with, 32–33. *See also* Friendships

Eastenson, A., 8, 13
Easton, D., 114
Eder, D., 78, 86, 98
Egan, S. K., 50
Elicker, J., 25
Enemies: avoidance of, 17–18; characteristics of, 8; children's negative evaluations of, 17–18; conceptualization of, 113; function of, 18–20; level of threat from, 8; methodological issues in study of, 11–13; perceived intent of, 17–18; perceptions of, 59, 61–62, 66–67; protectiveness of, 108; selection of, 20; similarity between, 117
Enemy relationships: analysis of relationship between adjustment and, 93–96; in attachment study, 26–32; behaviors as cause of, 89–90; and broken friendships, 33; as dyadic phenomena, 32; effects of, 89–90, 106–109; formation of, 13–16, 33–34; maintenance of, 16–18; prevalence of, 76–78; questions regarding formation of, 1; research needs in, 3. *See also* Enmities; Mutual antipathies
Englund, M., 25
Enmities: characteristics of, 8; definition of, 1; dyadic relationships' overlap with, 32–33; effect on behavior, 16; effect on friendships, 19; increased susceptibility to, 14–15; versus mutual antipathies, 8; versus rejection, 1–2; role of symmetry in formation of, 16. *See also* Enemy relationships
Ethnicity, 100–104
Evans, C. C., 78, 86

Fabes, R. A., 78
Falicov, C. J., 101
Family systems theory, 101
Farley, F. H., 51
Farmer, T. W., 2, 73, 113, 115, 116
Fathers, in attachment study, 26–32, 34–35
Furguson, T. J., 59
Fick, A. C., 39

Back Issue/Subscription Order Form

Copy or detach and send to:

Jossey-Bass, A Wiley Company, 989 Market Street, San Francisco CA 94103-1741

Call or fax toll-free: Phone 888-378-2537 6:30AM – 3PM PST; Fax 888-481-2665

Back Issues: Please send me the following issues at $29 each
(Important: please include series initials and issue number, such as CD99.)

_____

_____

_____

$ _____   Total for single issues

$ _____   SHIPPING CHARGES: SURFACE

	Domestic	Canadian
First Item	$5.00	$6.00
Each Add'l Item	$3.00	$1.50

For next-day and second-day delivery rates, call the number listed above.

Subscriptions: Please __start __renew my subscription to *New Directions for Child and Adolescent Development* for the year 2_____at the following rate:

U.S.	__Individual $90	__Institutional $195
Canada	__Individual $90	__Institutional $235
All Others	__Individual $114	__Institutional $269
Online Subscription		__Institutional $195

**For more information about online subscriptions visit
www.interscience.wiley.com**

$ _____   Total single issues and subscriptions (Add appropriate sales tax for your state for single issue orders. No sales tax for U.S. subscriptions. Canadian residents, add GST for subscriptions and single issues.)

__Payment enclosed (U.S. check or money order only)

__VISA __MC __AmEx # _____   Exp. Date _____

Signature _____ Day Phone _____

__ Bill Me (U.S. institutional orders only. Purchase order required.)

Purchase order # _____
                        Federal Tax ID13559302   GST 89102 8052

Name _____

Address _____

_____

Phone _____ E-mail _____

For more information about Jossey-Bass, visit our Web site at www.josseybass.com

OTHER TITLES AVAILABLE IN THE
NEW DIRECTIONS FOR CHILD AND ADOLESCENT DEVELOPMENT SERIES
William Damon, Editor-in-Chief

NEW DIRECTIONS FOR CHILD AND ADOLESCENT DEVELOPMENT IS NOW AVAILABLE ONLINE AT WILEY INTERSCIENCE

What is Wiley InterScience?

Wiley InterScience is the dynamic online content service from John Wiley & Sons delivering the full text of over 300 leading scientific, technical, medical, and professional journals, plus major reference works, the acclaimed Current Protocols laboratory manuals, and even the full text of select Wiley print books online.

What are some special features of Wiley InterScience?

Wiley Interscience Alerts is a service that delivers table of contents via e-mail for any journal available on Wiley InterScience as soon as a new issue is published online.

EarlyView is Wiley's exclusive service presenting individual articles online as soon as they are ready, even before the release of the compiled print issue. These articles are complete, peer-reviewed, and citable.

CrossRef is the innovative multi-publisher reference linking system enabling readers to move seamlessly from a reference in a journal article to the cited publication, typically located on a different server and published by a different publisher.

How can I access Wiley InterScience?

Visit http://www.interscience.wiley.com.

Guest Users can browse Wiley InterScience for unrestricted access to journal tables of contents and article abstracts, or use the powerful search engine.

Registered Users are provided with a *Personal Home Page* to store and manage customized alerts, searches, and links to favorite journals and articles. Additionally, Registered Users can view free online sample issues and preview selected material from major reference works.

Licensed Customers are entitled to access full-text journal articles in PDF, with select journals also offering full-text HTML.

How do I become an Authorized User?

Authorized Users are individuals authorized by a paying Customer to have access to the journals in Wiley InterScience. For example, a university that subscribes to Wiley journals is considered to be the Customer.

Faculty, staff and students authorized by the university to have access to those journals in Wiley InterScience are Authorized Users. Users should contact their library for information on which Wiley journals they have access to in Wiley InterScience.

ASK YOUR INSTITUTION ABOUT WILEY INTERSCIENCE TODAY!

United States Postal Service

Statement of Ownership, Management, and Circulation

1. Publication Title	2. Publication Number	3. Filing Date
New Directions For Child And Adolescent Development	1 5 2 0 - 3 2 4 7	9/30/03

4. Issue Frequency	5. Number of Issues Published Annually	6. Annual Subscription Price
Quarterly	4	$90 Individual $195 Institution

7. Complete Mailing Address of Known Office of Publication (Not printer) (Street, city, county, state, and ZIP+4)

989 Market Street
San Francisco, CA 94103-1741

San Francisco County

Contact Person: Joe Schuman

Telephone: 415 782 3232

8. Complete Mailing Address of Headquarters or General Business Office of Publisher (Not printer)

Same as above

9. Full Names and Complete Mailing Addresses of Publisher, Editor, and Managing Editor (Do not leave blank)

Publisher (Name and complete mailing address)

Wiley, San Francisco
Jossey-Bass - Pfeiffer
Address - same as above

Editor (Name and complete mailing address)

William Damon
Stanford Center On Adolescence
Cypress Bldg. C Stanford University
Stanford, CA 94305-4145

Managing Editor (Name and complete mailing address)

None

10. Owner (Do not leave blank. If the publication is owned by a corporation, give the name and address of the corporation immediately followed by the names and addresses of all stockholders owning or holding 1 percent or more of the total amount of stock. If not owned by a corporation, give the names and addresses of the individual owners. If owned by a partnership or other unincorporated firm, give its name and address as well as those of each individual owner. If the publication is published by a nonprofit organization, give its name and address.)

Full Name	Complete Mailing Address
John Wiley & Sons Inc.	111 River Street Hoboken, NJ 07030

11. Known Bondholders, Mortgagees, and Other Security Holders Owning or Holding 1 Percent or More of Total Amount of Bonds, Mortgages, or Other Securities. If none, check box ☐ None

Full Name	Complete Mailing Address
Same as above	Same as above

12. Tax Status (For completion by nonprofit organizations authorized to mail at nonprofit rates) (Check one)
The purpose, function, and nonprofit status of this organization and the exempt status for federal income tax purposes:
☐ Has Not Changed During Preceding 12 Months
☐ Has Changed During Preceding 12 Months (Publisher must submit explanation of change with this statement)

PS Form 3526, October 1999   (See Instructions on Reverse)

---

13. Publication Title	14. Issue Date for Circulation Data Below
New Directions For Child And Adolescent Development	Summer 2003

15.	Extent and Nature of Circulation	Average No. Copies Each Issue During Preceding 12 Months	No. Copies of Single Issue Published Nearest to Filing Date
a.	Total Number of Copies (Net press run)	1,040	972
b. Paid and/or Requested Circulation	(1) Paid/Requested Outside-County Mail Subscriptions Stated on Form 3541 (Include advertiser's proof and exchange copies)	347	350
	(2) Paid In-County Subscriptions Stated on Form 3541 (Include advertiser's proof and exchange copies)	0	0
	(3) Sales Through Dealers and Carriers, Street Vendors, Counter Sales, and Other Non-USPS Paid Distribution	0	0
	(4) Other Classes Mailed Through the USPS	0	0
c.	Total Paid and/or Requested Circulation (Sum of 15b. (1), (2),(3),and (4)) ▶	347	350
d. Free Distribution by Mail (Samples, complimentary, and other free)	(1) Outside-County as Stated on Form 3541	0	0
	(2) In-County as Stated on Form 3541	0	0
	(3) Other Classes Mailed Through the USPS	1	1
e.	Free Distribution Outside the Mail (Carriers or other means)	75	77
f.	Total Free Distribution (Sum of 15d. and 15e.) ▶	76	78
g.	Total Distribution (Sum of 15c. and 15f.) ▶	423	428
h.	Copies not Distributed	617	544
i.	Total (Sum of 15g. and h.) ▶	1,040	972
j.	Percent Paid and/or Requested Circulation (15c. divided by 15g. times 100)	82%	82%

16. Publication of Statement of Ownership
☐ Publication required. Will be printed in the Winter 2003 issue of this publication.   ☐ Publication not required.

17. Signature and Title of Editor, Publisher, Business Manager, or Owner

Susan E. Lewis
VP & Publisher - Periodicals

Date 9/30/03

I certify that all information furnished on this form is true and complete. I understand that anyone who furnishes false or misleading information on this form or who omits material or information requested on the form may be subject to criminal sanctions (including fines and imprisonment) and/or civil sanctions (including civil penalties).

Instructions to Publishers

1. Complete and file one copy of this form with your postmaster annually on or before October 1. Keep a copy of the completed form for your records.

2. In cases where the stockholder or security holder is a trustee, include in items 10 and 11 the name of the person or corporation for whom the trustee is acting. Also include the names and addresses of individuals who are stockholders who own or hold 1 percent or more of the total amount of bonds, mortgages, or other securities of the publishing corporation. In item 11, if none, check the box. Use blank sheets if more space is required.

3. Be sure to furnish all circulation information called for in item 15. Free circulation must be shown in items 15d, e, and f.

4. Item 15h., Copies not Distributed, must include (1) newsstand copies originally stated on Form 3541, and returned to the publisher, (2) estimated returns from news agents, and (3), copies for office use, leftovers, spoiled, and all other copies not distributed.

5. If the publication had Periodicals authorization as a general or requester publication, this Statement of Ownership, Management, and Circulation must be published; it must be printed in any issue in October or, if the publication is not published during October, the first issue printed after October.

6. In item 16, indicate the date of the issue in which this Statement of Ownership will be published.

7. Item 17 must be signed.

Failure to file or publish a statement of ownership may lead to suspension of Periodicals authorization.

PS Form 3526, October 1999 (Reverse)